2 WEEKS

IW

CULTIVATING
SACRED SPACE
GARDENING FOR THE SOUL

Elizabeth Murray

Pomegranate

San Francisco

Published by Pomegranate
Box 6099, Rohnert Park, California 94927

Pomegranate Europe Ltd.
Fullbridge House, Fullbridge
Maldon, Essex CM9 7LE, England

Endpaper illustrations by Elizabeth Murray
Apple tree paper silhouettes by Robin Goodfellow
Garden illustration by Terry Wilson
Cover and interior design by Publication Design and Production, Santa Rosa, CA

Pomegranate Catalog No. A901

Library of Congress Cataloging-in-Publication Data

Murray, Elizabeth, 1953–
      Cultivating sacred space : gardening for the soul / Elizabeth
Murray. -- 1st ed.
          p.   cm.
      Includes bibliographical references.
      ISBN 0-7649-0360-8 (hardcover : alk. paper)
      1. Gardening.   2. Gardens.   3. Gardening--Religious aspects.
   4. Gardens--Religious aspects.   5. Gardens--Symbolic aspects.
   6. Seasons.   I. Title.
   SB455.M87   1997
   635'.01--dc21   97-14724
                                                              CIP

Printed in Hong Kong
06 05 04 03 02 01 00 99 98 97   10 9 8 7 6 5 4 3 2 1

First Edition

This book is lovingly dedicated to my husband, Gerald Bol, whose loving kindness and creative, generous, and adventurous spirit have enriched my soul forever. Gerald, you showed me by your courageous example to live what you believe, even in the wars of cancer. I offer this book as a healing tale of love, courage, and continuum.

Elizabeth Murray

Contents

Introduction

The garden has always been my personal sanctuary—a place for my soul to be nurtured. When I was a child, we had a very old apple tree in our backyard garden. My brothers and sisters and I cherished this humble little tree, which taught us about the changing of seasons. In winter, we saw how strong and beautiful her bare limbs were. In spring, she gave us pink blossoms, and my pet rabbits and I played under her branches. In summer, she gave us shade; in autumn, apples to eat and piles of leaves to crunch. Our great-aunt and grandmother told us stories of the fairies and little people who would come to live under the tree if we took good care of the garden and believed. There is much more to a garden than meets the eye, and like the fairies and the unseen roots, its deepest source of sustenance, magic, or balance is not often visible.

All parts of a tree speak. The roots tell about the dark underground life in the soil—like our own soul life—that sustains growth. The trunk holds the heart of the here and now of daily life, connecting the two realms. The crown resides—like the birds and the angels up in the sky, like our spirits—transforming light into life. And each season brings us in touch with the cycles and rhythms of life and our own wild, ever-connected soul nature.

Echoing Nature's cycle, this book is my reflection on the garden and on life, season by season. We begin with winter, the time of dormancy and going inward, the quiet, reflective, bare-bones part of the year. This is the season for pruning out dead wood and bringing precious illumination to the dark night of our souls.

Spring is the time of regeneration and blossoming. In this section I have gathered and intuited about one hundred archetypes that relate to the garden. Such archetypes bring ancient meaning to sacred space, enabling us to cultivate our soil/soul more deeply and richly.

Summer is the time of expansion. Here I present twelve sacred spaces, each completely different and each made with love and intention. Every one of these gardens expands the definition of "sacred space" and inspires us to express our own unique and authentic voice.

Autumn is the time of fruition and harvest, when we celebrate the fruits of our cultivation. It is a powerful act to create personal ceremonies and celebrations that will imbue our spaces with love, grace, and memory. It is not enough to fill a space with symbolic objects, even objects of great beauty. The vitality of a space comes with use—with play, song, and ritual.

Three years ago, on my way to Bali, I sent my "Sacred Space" manuscript to my publisher. After more than four years of work, I thought it was complete; my trip was a treasured reward for my efforts. Through their immense creativity and direct intimacy with Nature, the Balinese opened my heart to the sacred in everyday life. My soul was enriched to the very root of my being.

On my return, I met up with Gerald Bol, who had been my art teacher and mentor when I was twenty-one, and we fell deeply in love. As artists and gardeners, Gerald and I had much to share, and we happily began to redesign our lives so that we could be together as much as possible. Gerald's wife of twenty-four years had died the previous year from breast cancer, the same disease that had claimed both my mother and my sister-in-law. We had both walked the path of death with our loved ones; through the transformative fire of loss and grief, we had gained a glimmering of something eternal in our own souls, something that can never be lost or destroyed. We also knew how short life is, how unpredictable—and yet, with love, how very precious. As Gerald and I grew closer, it became important to me to have his response to my manuscript, so I read it aloud to him. In his kind and supportive way, he gently pointed out that although the book had much to offer, it depended too much on quotes from other writers. "Your voice is important, Lizzie," he said, "and the quotes disrupt your flow."

It was primarily through my profound life experiences with Gerald that I was able to reenvision this book, to find my voice again, and begin anew. Much of this reemergence was directly connected to the love, creative vision, and garden Gerald and I made together. Just as we all can find joy and nourishment in our gardens—by digging deep into the earth, pruning, planting, weeding, rediscovering—so can we revel in the beauty, mystery, and challenges of our lives. The garden has always been a vehicle for me to connect with my soul. It provides me with spiritual sustenance, just as the soil sustains the plants that flourish within it.

I have written *Cultivating Sacred Space: Gardening for the Soul* with much guidance and inspiration, received in many forms and with great appreciation. The process has been a living, growing one. I hope that in reading this book you are taken on a journey of discovery and heart opening as rich as the one I have had in writing it.

WINTER

I n winter our gardens, like we ourselves, must have the will and determination to make it through the months of darkness—to face the cold and wind and yet survive. Patience is required during these dormant times, as well as trust that transformation is taking place and that spring will come again. When I lived in France in 1985 the winter was so terribly cold, and all the plants around me seemed lifeless. I felt very lonely and isolated. When the buds began to swell on the willow

MONET'S POND IN WINTER

Giverny, France

trees, I took heart and searched the ground to find some green sprouts pushing up. Just as candlelight seems so much warmer and brighter in winter—when sunlight is scarce each small flame is so appreciated—snowdrop flowers seem especially welcome and bright, softly whispering reminders of life under the blanket of cold, crushing snow. Their power and pluck, beauty and light, can kindle the human spirit.

Winter is a time of purification, cleansing, making space for the new to arise. Winter storms can cause great destruction, including flooding and rock slides, and even cause precious, magnificent old trees to come down. When such a tree falls we are forced to confront change—like the sudden illness or death of a loved one. Decisions must be made about what to do with the tree, how to use it, and how the garden must now adjust to the empty space and new source of light. When the Dalai Lama was asked how he could withstand the loss of so many of his friends—a million Tibetans were killed by Chinese troops in 1959—he said that the loss of a friend brings sadness for a time, but then there is room for new friends. This is faith in continuum: that more friends will come, and the love and memory of those gone are still with us. The felled tree can make room for new plants, like new friends. Plus, the dead tree can become useful in itself—as a bench for contemplation, as firewood for warmth, as food for all kinds of life.

Winter is a time of evaluation. Looking at the bare bones bereft of flesh, we can better see the structure and decide if it can support our intentions, or if it needs modification. At this time of year it is valuable to go over garden journals and photos to decide what things we did well the previous year and want to maintain and repeat, and what can be improved. I do this for the new year, letting go of any pain, bad habits, or negative thinking, and bringing with me appreciation for the goodness, love, and growth I experienced as well. This is especially important when something traumatic has occurred, like the loss of a great tree in the garden or a loved one in our life—to bring their love and memory along with us into the new year.

Winter, cold and dark, is a time to experience the empty space, to embark on our personal journey, to look for our star. This is the story of the Magi, the magic ones, who were guided by a star to find the birth of Pure Love. The light we all long for, seek, and need, especially at this time of year, is more than the sunlight—it is the illumination and warmth of love. That is why the hospitality of a friend's hearth and his or her loving embrace mean so much to us, especially during the dark times. We welcome the light to warm us and help our plants to grow. We carefully prune the trees to allow more light to find its way in. We cherish the sunny spots—gentle, luminous light gives a radiant warmth and comfort.

Still we must trust the goings on and stirrings under the earth. We need not dig up the seeds and shine a light on them to see if they are indeed growing. They need their quiet, restful time of darkness to send out their roots. There are times in our life for acceptance and nurture, when digging up the psyche is inappropriate and can even disturb growth. And there are times in our gardens for contemplation, rest, and dormancy.

Gardening for soul enrichment—purification, evaluation, experiencing the empty space—is a completely different approach than gardening to satisfy the ego. King Louis XIV, for example, gardened for his ego; his gardens at Versailles showed his power and wealth. He had villages razed to open vistas for his garden views, hundreds of gardeners, and dozens of fountains. There was not enough water pressure, however, to have all of these many fountains flowing at once. When he strolled the gardens, workers had to run covertly behind him turning off the fountain he had just seen while others ahead were quickly turning on the one he was about to see. All an illusion.

Our soul needs authenticity—the real thing —but with kindness and gentleness, not harshness. Sometimes illusions are chosen to project a different persona, to veil the truth. But when many veils are layered on, our sight can be obscured and we can lose track of who we really are. A bit of bird netting over a tree can preserve the fruit from birds, but too much will inhibit the tree's growth. With a close friend, authenticity is required so that real love will flourish.

If a hungry friend came and knocked at your door on a cold night, you would graciously welcome her in, sit her by the fire, help her shed her wet, clumsy clothes. You'd give her a blanket to wrap herself in and hot soup and drink to warm and nourish herself. Then, when she was rested, well fed, and comfortable, her story might emerge. Your hospitality, your love and acceptance would soothe your friend, and the soft warm light of your hearth would pull her out of her dark night. This is what our soul asks us to do for ourselves when we are spiritually hungry.

My sacred space gives me this kind of nurturing. I light candles and a fire and hold in memory my great love, who has passed on. Sometimes I must cover up and go into solitude and silence and trust that growth will come after this cold, dormant time. It's like when I plant and cover the bulbs and seeds with soil, committing them to the darkness with the faith that, at the right time, when the soil is warmed they will grow.

If we were to greet our friend at the door with impatient questions of "What are you doing here?" and "What's wrong?"—questions from the fearful ego rather than the hospitable heart that accepts and welcomes—our friend would leave hurt and despondent, not full and cared for. Patience, warmth, and sustenance will bring about the growth we desire in our friends, our bulbs, our souls.

Our gardens can teach us a lot about patience. Indeed, gardens grown without patience all look alike: fast-growing, overfertilized lawns and shrubs, and impatient flowers. My friend Mme. Mallet, who is well into her eighties, once said to me while gesturing to her garden, Parc des Moutiers, now nearly a century old, "It's just now getting good, isn't it, Elizabeth?" This woman has been rewarded by her patience and her vision. She then pointed to a new grove of blue cedar trees she had just planted to give structure in the future, another gesture of faith and commitment to continuum. (Parc des Moutiers is featured on the dust jacket of this book.)

Faith is expressed by the soul gardener who trusts the dormancy, the fallow times. Treasure the emergence and be gentle and protective of your soul during adverse conditions. There will be a flourishing.

Awakening

A sensual garden can awaken our connections to the sacred. The Celtic mystic Father John O'Donahue says that our senses are "the gateway to the soul." In looking outward to a beautiful flower, our eye is delighted, but we are also touched inside our hearts, as Nature is a direct expression of the divine. It is a contemplative act to do a repetitive action like weeding, which involves sight (which little green sprout is a weed and which a flower?), touch (get a good hold!), and smell (moist, aromatic earth and budding flowers). Each of our five senses plays an important part in our discovery of the sacred, and they can be stimulated in winter as well as in the other seasons.

Smell. Tending our gardens is an outward, physical action that unites body, mind, and spirit. It is like breathing. Taking in air brings us energy, and exhaling releases tensions and promotes letting go and trusting in the next breath. The simple rhythm of successive breaths is both life-sustaining and transformational, connecting us to the air, the sky, the heavens. When there is a pleasant fragrance in the air our sense of smell is awakened. Scent is our strongest connection to memory, and memories are the treasures of life—making us the unique individuals we are. The smell of a rose can link us up with memories—from our grandmother's garden to our first Valentine's bouquet—and the herb rosemary stimulates memory directly and is used in aromatherapy.

Touch. When we prune, plant, weed, and harvest we are touching the soil, the plants, and the tools. I like to include plants in my garden that are purely sensual to the touch (soft velvety lamb's ear is one of my favorites). As with a person, there are different ways to touch plants and different feelings thereby expressed. Usually a gentle touch expresses love and care, and we feel comforted. A caress from a lover can stimulate our whole body. Touch can immediately connect our bodies to our feelings and our sense of well being; it connects us to our inner selves. Our language begins to develop, our communication deepens and becomes more fluid. We say we are deeply "touched" when our hearts open. Touching plants, especially mature trees, can connect us to Nature more intimately and help us develop our relationship and feelings for these beautiful natural beings.

Taste. Our sense of taste can easily be stimulated by the fruits, vegetables, herbs, and edible flowers in the garden. This is an especially direct connection between Nature and our entire body. I felt such a deeply meaningful and delightful communion one time standing with my little five-year-old niece, Rebecca, and friends around a generous raspberry patch, eating those divine berry gems. Our delight and appreciation was felt in every flavor-filled, melt-in-your-mouth berry. What better way could there be to develop good taste!

Hearing. In our gardens, our own personal sanctuaries, we can be fulfilled by silence. The silence in a garden is not an empty, hollow, lonely silence—it is a soft silence that gently beckons us to go inward into our own souls. A great stone in the garden can teach a lot about the beauty and groundedness of silence. In fact, as in ancient Chinese and Japanese gardens, a well-chosen stone can be a focal point for meditation. I listen to music in the garden when I want to stay outward and be entertained and just get the job at hand completed. But when my soul yearns to be tended, I go into the garden to cultivate both my inner and outer life—to silently build a bridge from the seen world to the unseen. The silence is then enriching and enables me to walk along an inner path that, with my usual distractions, I may never have noticed otherwise. I also have purposely placed a beautiful-sounding wind chime in the garden which occasionally and spontaneously sings to me. The lingering vibrations of its harmonic sound resonate within me and, like a musical string finely tuned, I find myself coming into harmony with this inward and outward rhythm.

Sight. To truly see the beauty of every nuance of light, color, and texture in our intimate sacred gardens—to gaze deeply and see well—is to bring a plant or quality of light—or even a person—deep into our souls. We have the opportunity to develop our vision—to be visionary—to know the visible and invisible worlds. We can have intimate insights like a macro lens for detail while at the same time hold the distant and the overall views to see the whole picture.

In our gardens as well as in our daily life, each perspective of inner and outer detail as well as the wide-angle view is vital and richly fulfilling. Photography has been a spiritual tool for me to train my eye to really see and take in—to record on film different points of view and different moments of light and illumination. The practice of photography, still a magical alchemy, gives me clear sight as well as deep insight. I am forever humbled and rewarded with both photography and gardening.

Relationship and Reflection

Most of us long for connectedness and deep relationships, and some of us fear change as a threat to our sense of security and stability. Our gardens can provide a place of deep connection and belonging, where we can express our personal identities and form relationships with our space, our plants, and ourselves. Additionally, change is something we actually look forward to in a garden: the first shoots from the spring bulbs, the trees beginning to blossom, and the change of green foliage into fire tones in autumn. We "lose" something to "gain" something else. The striking silhouette of a bare apple tree disappears with the advent of delicate pink blossoms, which give way to the coming of the harvest.

In the garden we can experience the connectedness and trust in change—and even death—because there is a continuum; there are no final endings. Even when a plant is pulled out, it can go into the compost pile to transform into the riches that renew the soil. We can find much comfort and depth of experience in our gardens.

The gardener has a relationship with the garden, and each reflects and nurtures the other. When the garden is young it requires more time to develop—to be visited, noticed, listened to. There is an exchange. A good relationship offers interchange for the enrichment of all. Yet good intentions alone do not feed the soil/soul. Sometimes it is the deep digging—the turning over of the dark depths—that makes for more sustained growth. Sometimes weeding is required—our eye must focus to recognize the desired from the undesired, and then comes the action—the actual work. Making the time to weed gives us the space we need to thrive. Our lives are so crowded with obligations and busyness, but if we don't do regular weeding, our growth is hindered (remember the expression, "weeding is a gardener's meditation").

When too much of a good thing comes up, thinning is required for the garden to develop fully. I've always so much wanted it all, to do it all—to not miss anything. But as I mature, I'm learning the importance of discrimination, to make choices and provide myself enough space and time.

Most plants benefit from pinching out the

terminal bud. This encourages the plant to branch out, to become fuller and more well-rounded, rather than growing quickly in only one direction. My life pinches me on a regular basis. I've grown in so many directions, I am quite full and bushy. Sometimes, of course, I yearn to be the slender vine, reaching out to only one direction.

Pruning is necessary for plants that grow more than one season. Trees and shrubs that live a long time need guidance. The gardener is the guide. I used to think of pruning as an arduous task, the sooner completed, the better. Then an older woman gardener told me it was her favorite job because it required vision. Before making a cut, we must assess the entire plant and look for crossed branches (growth in opposite directions), a crowded crown, or a sick limb, cane, or branch. We cut out dead wood, excess that is no longer serving us. Then we cut out entanglements that inhibit our growth. We prune for openness—an airy plant with plenty of light will not invite pests and diseases. I try to prune to stimulate the growth of buds that will grow in a desired direction. Overall balance, health, and beauty are my pruning goals, always respecting and preserving the unique character and growth habit of the plant as well as my desire. This is what I strive for in my own life as well.

Roots sprout first. This gives the seed the ability to be stable and nurture itself before it shows itself above ground. The stronger the roots, the more developed and nourished, the greater the outer growth will be. I've seen many quickly grown plants that have even reached full bloom wither and die suddenly. When I pull up such plants to check their roots, I find they were insufficient to sustain all the top growth. Sometimes the roots have been eaten by a gopher. Sometimes the plants have been pushed to bloom by an impatient nurseryman or overwatered by an anxious gardener. Overwatering, especially without good drainage, will rot the roots. The top of the plant will be stressed, limp, and appear to be lacking water; but the plant is suffering from thirst because the damaged roots cannot take the water up, even when it is available. To be well rooted is to have good health. To be well rooted, yet flexible, is to be like the bamboo.

Our soul must be like the bamboo. A deep, strong root system will help us weather the difficulties of life, but we must avoid rigidity in the way we think and live. Nutrients must be available to feed and sustain us. Creativity, like moisture, is essential, keeping us juicy and flowing. Light and warmth, patience and acceptance are necessities for growth. Fresh air breezes take away stagnant thinking.

Good drainage is required to allow excesses to flow away. A plant in a pot without a hole or in clay soil with poor drainage will hold the water and will eventually drown. Tight containers bind the roots so they go around and around in circles, never able to push out and explore new ground. Then the roots become very dependent on regular watering because no taproot has been established to go to a deeper source for nourishment. Growth is limited. A good gardener will gently loosen the roots and provide an extra large hole full of nutrients to encourage good growth and lessen transplant shock. Strong roots provide plants stability during storms; fierce winds usually cannot knock down plants with well-established roots. When plants are transplanted it is important to help them adjust to their new climate, soil, and conditions, allowing time for rest.

When I plant I try to follow the old gardener's advice: "It's better to put a $1 plant in a $5 hole than a $5 plant in a $1 hole." In other words, a carefully prepared and well-selected spot to live will allow the most modest plant to thrive; whereas a larger, more expensive plant will suffer if the preparation is poor. I too, of course, grow best where all my needs are met.

Many new gardeners find it so frustrating to spend so much time, money, and hard work on the soil—something that doesn't even show. Likewise, some people when depressed will buy a lot of new clothes to look good, rather than do deep soul work—which doesn't show as readily. I've always been one to dig deep in the muck, adding my own composted materials. I have noticed over the years that though I've grown more slowly (and at times have felt like a late

bloomer), my inner soul garden and outer landscape gardens tend to flourish over time. The growth not only catches up with more "instantly installed" gardens, but matures gracefully with age, becoming only more beautiful.

People are amazed to see eight-foot-high foxgloves and twelve-foot-tall hollyhocks waving in each of the new gardens I've planted. They grow this dynamically because of all the deep soil work I've done in preparation. This is what has made me feel at home. When I move, I usually grieve for the garden I left behind, my friends, my own rootedness that is in transplant shock. If I can, I bring some potted plants or some cuttings with me. When I last left my garden to start a new life with my husband, Gerald, I brought some of my scented geranium cuttings. The children and I call them magic leaves, because they smell like lemons, roses, or green apples. The climate was different in my new garden, so my geraniums didn't thrive immediately. They were in danger of freezing in the winter without special care. On a cold night I put flannel sheets on them for protection (the sheets smelled great in the morning), but I had to bring them inside to winter over. I realized, too, that I was not growing the same. I wasn't yet well rooted. I needed extra attention and care—because this new environment required so much more of me. The nature of the place was not the same. It was a wilder place, less tended. It did not at first contain my vision and my soul, which came later with Gerald's and my combined investment of time, love, and work. Then the garden was far greater than we could have created alone.

Every garden requires love and vision. Like a child, it needs to be nurtured and understood for its own potential. When young, children and gardens require some structure and then must be allowed to go a bit wild; to self-seed and clamber around, finding their own expression and direction. This is how they retain their own spirit and individuality. This is the way to full flourishing. And this spirit of place and free spirit in place—reflections of nature—can only thrive with nurture and freedom.

Illustrations of Illuminations

I hope the following illuminating artworks will feed your soul over winter and fill you with inspiration—like the seed catalogs that we pore over by our hearths, filling our hearts and minds with visions of what could be, what might emerge from our own soil. These paintings chart the connections between garden makers and lovers, real and imagined, throughout many centuries. Take them into your dreams so they can come through your soul into your own sacred space.

TREE OF LIFE
EIGHTEENTH-CENTURY INDIAN TEXTILE

Courtesy Winterthur Museum

The ancient archetype of the Tree of Life predates the Christian myth of the Tree of Knowledge in the garden of Eden. Eating the apple from the Tree of Knowledge allowed Adam and Eve to know the difference between good and evil, which led to their expulsion from Paradise, where the existence of evil had been unknown to them. True knowledge of life includes the dark side, the unconscious realms, the dream life, the acceptance of the life-death-life cycle. The tree has been used to symbolize this because it lives in all three realms of reality. Its roots are underground in the darkness, symbolically in the unconscious, the source of enrichment and nourishment. The trunk is the central axis, the link, the body and strength of the here and now. The tree's crown reaches into the cosmos. It can look down at the trunk and roots and become conscious of itself, like in a spiritual practice. The leaves alchemically transform air and light into food, for the tree as well as the fruit, for enrichment and continuum. The tree connects the underworld with the earth and heavens.

The Tree of Life forms a spiral up and down a central axis, becoming an *axis mundi* extending from heaven to earth, recalling ancient symbols for eternity. Yet, unlike a spiral, which extends indefinitely in both directions, the Tree of Life is a

finite whole, a complete organism. Like the Eastern yin-yang sign, the Tree of Life symbolizes the darkness which is a part of the light and the light which is a part of the darkness; each flows into the other to make up the whole.

According to anthropologist Angeles Arrien, trees are the medicine people of the plant world among many indigenous cultures. The roots are associated with the past, ancestors, and dream work. The trunk is the present and like the heart, it connects the deep-rooted, ancient knowing with the crown, the far-reaching dreams and goals. When there is health, balance, and vitality, the strong trunk is an effective transmitter of energy and support for both realms. Then fruition can occur.

The two vases embroidered on this Tree of Life textile are more than decorative. They symbolize abundant life springing forth, the water of life. The vase is a symbol of fertility and creativity, like the womb. This Tree of Life depicts many different fruits, flowers, and leaves, reminding us that a rich life is full of diversity. The central pomegranate is another ancient symbol for fertility's possibility. The sweet, juicy seeds provide life and sustenance in an otherwise arid climate, like the pomegranate seeds that nurtured Persephone in the underworld when she was abducted by Hades. The seeds gave her sustenance, but ever-linked her to the dark side. According to the myth, winter and dormancy on earth were thus created, as a result of Persephone's annual passage to the underworld. Spring and rebirth occur with her return to earth. Both the dark and light are needed for life and new growth.

The Tree of Life simultaneously reaches heavenward and deep into the earth, or underworld. It creates food alchemically from the dark earth and the sunlight, that is, through photosynthesis. In Sufi tradition, "the Verdant One" represents the green life forms on earth and is personified by Khidir, who is dressed in robes the color of light coming through green foliage—the "green gold" the Renaissance alchemists tried to make. Like the icon of mother and child, the Tree of Life is the blending of earthly soul life with celestial spirit life coming into fruition.

CULTIVATING
SACRED SPACE

ILLUSTRATION FROM "THE SONG OF LOS"
BY WILLIAM BLAKE, 1795

COLOR PRINT WITH WATERCOLOR, PEN AND INK

*The Huntington Library, Art Collections and Botanical Gardens,
San Marino, California*

Song is a sacred tool for finding our own voice and connecting heart and mind. There are songs that open and heal our hearts, like many love songs, and there are songs that connect us to our spirits and souls, like spirituals and Gospel songs. We teach small children songs for play and learning, and we use marching songs for strength, bravery, and courage. We need to sing to open our hearts and call in our good intentions, to bless both the sacred space of our garden and ourselves, the creators. It is essential for each of us to find and use our own unique voice, to bring healing to ourselves as well as the earth.

This painting is of Los, the male muse sitting over the world. He is similar in function and symbolism to Khidir, "the Verdant One." Blake has illustrated his mythological poem to show how creativity prevails over reason and law. He asserts the artist's rights to his own personal visions. Imagination gives its force to technique. In creating our own gardens we have the opportunity to let our imaginations go free—to play out and develop our own unique ideas and personal visions. By creating a sacred garden, we can increase our awareness and respect for the spirit and interconnectedness in all of Nature.

"JALAL BEFORE THE MYSTICAL TREE"
FIFTEENTH-CENTURY PERSIAN MINIATURE

Courtesy Uppsala Universitetsbibliotek, Sweden

This fifteenth-century Persian miniature tells the story of Jalal, whose name means "Glory" and who is seeking the love of Jamal, the daughter of Mihrarai, the king of the angelic beings. Jalal is a mystic, and his quest for wholeness is an allegory of love. On his journey he enters into a delightful garden where flowers speak to him and his name is written on the leaves of a miraculous tree. Jamal, whose name means "Beauty," appears to him fleetingly in the form of different birds. We can find wholeness and balance in our own spirit through beauty and love. In the garden every flower and leaf and living creature will speak to us of beauty and connect us to the spirit in all of life, expressed in the miraculous ways of Nature, opening our hearts to love. The pursuit of beauty in all things and the creation of beauty in our daily life is a sacred act. It is a way of life that connects us to the divine.

CULTIVATING
SACRED SPACE

"LOVERS PICNICKING"
SIXTEENTH-CENTURY PERSIAN MINIATURE,
ATTRIBUTED TO SULTAN-MUHAMMAD

Private collection;
photograph courtesy Harvard University Art Museums

Here is another Persian miniature wherein love flourishes in an ancient garden. Love, the emblem for wholeness, is achieved in an environment invested with beauty and the stimulation of all senses. All the pleasures of Paradise—flowering trees, meadows, delicious food and drink, music, and dancing—surround this couple. Their love is nurtured by their radiant environment. There is an ever-fulfilling flow of beauty and love between the lovers and the garden. This is the quality in a garden that can bring a sense of renewal to our own lives as well as to our communities. Natural beauty can fill a yearning in all of us, but especially in those of us in large cities, which are more distant from Nature and crowded with humanity and pavement. All personal expressions of love, creativity, and beauty can breathe new life into any harsh environment in the acts of creating as well as in receiving the beauty. Lily Yeh's gardens in Philadelphia are a radiant example (see pages 124–131).

"NYMPHÉAS, WATER LANDSCAPE"
BY CLAUDE MONET, 1907
OIL ON CANVAS

Wadsworth Atheneum, Hartford. Bequest of Anne Parrish Titzell

Monet created his water lily garden for beauty and his own enrichment. What he found was endless inspiration and tranquility. His greatest passion was painting the fleeting quality of the light. He could sit tirelessly and contemplate the clouds reflecting on his blooming mirror. Monet was inspired to paint hundreds of canvases of these ever-changing effects of light,

which he imbued with his sense of awe and reverence for Nature.

Through Monet's intimate observations of the light on his pond, he experienced the transformations of time. It was his spiritual meditation to record the temporal impressions of the kaleidoscopic mirages and reflections. Monet spoke of the total self-surrender he gave to his work and likened it to that of the monks who painted the illuminated books of hours. "These [illuminated books] owe everything to the collaboration of solitude and passion, to an earnest, exclusive attention bordering on hypnosis. . . . The richness I achieve comes from Nature, the source of my inspiration."[1]

CULTIVATING
SACRED SPACE

---

[1]*As quoted by Roger Marx in his article "Les Nymphéas de M. Claude Monet," Gazette des Beaux Arts, series 4, Vol. 1, June 1909.*

"A YOUNG DAUGHTER OF THE PICTS"
BY JACQUES LE MOYNE DE MORGUES,
c. 1585
WATERCOLOR AND BODY COLOR TOUCHED
WITH GOLD, ON VELLUM
Yale Center for British Art, Paul Mellon Collection

Here is a woman truly celebrating the beauty and bounty of the earth. The Picts were Celts from ancient Scotland. Their name comes from the Latin *pictus,* "pictures," because they completely tattooed their bodies with images of magical beauty—flowers, birds, beasts, and fish belonging to the Great Mother. These powerful women were shamans, visionaries, and healers. They also ritually initiated and taught the Celtic warrior-heroes the sacred mysteries of sexuality and power. They were known for their great physical strength and bravery as they led the Celtic tribes into battle, wearing only their tattooed flowers and swords. This woman reminds us to have the courage to fully develop ourselves to be warriors, teachers, healers, and visionaries—the way of the fourfold path as cited by Angeles Arrien.

CULTIVATING
SACRED SPACE

Uffizi Gallery, Florence, Italy
Photograph courtesy Erich Lessing/Art Resource, New York

In the center of these enchanted gardens is Venus, the goddess of Love and Beauty, who is blessing spring. Spring for the Romans was associated with renewal, fertility, and reawakening. In this image, forty-two varieties of wildflowers flourish under her feet, and sweet golden oranges hang ripe in the trees above her head. The wild and the cultivated flourish together to nurture body and soul. Mercury, on the far left, holds back the clouds and guards the three Graces, who dance in a circle with hands joined. They embody and celebrate the beauty created by Venus. At the far right, Zephyrus, the wind god, breathes life into Chloris, who then transforms into Flora (Primavera), goddess of spring, flowers, and gardens.

The wind bringing life to Chloris reminds me of what Chief Seattle said: "The wind also gives our children the spirit of Life." From the name "Chloris" comes *chlorophyll,* the green plant energy that transforms sun, air, and water into food for the plant (a plant with *chlorosis* is too yellow and lacks energy). From the goddess Flora we use the botanical term *floridus,* which means "free flowering." Since ancient times the garden has been the place for beauty, creativity, energy, diversity, and transformational renewal.

CULTIVATING
SACRED SPACE

SPRING

Spring is the time of regeneration of new life and sacred beginnings. I love the spring. I was born on Easter Sunday and always associate my birthday with bright green grassy hills covered with blue lupine and golden California poppies. In these beloved hills we would search for Easter eggs. The egg, like a flower bulb, symbolizes new life emerging from dormancy, like Christ rising from his tomb to demonstrate that life continues after death.

❋

APPLE TREES IN FULL BLOOM

Portland, Oregon

Springtime is so fresh and new it feels like the youngest season. Delicate blossoms pop from old woody branches. We feel an inner longing for sowing of seeds and falling in love. Potential flows with the warming of the soil in our garden and the renewal of our own souls. This is a time of celebration, including dancing around the maypole—the pagan fertility ritual.

At this time of year, when even Mother Nature renews herself with beautiful fresh new leaves and flowers, I want to share some ancient archetypal symbols and some old arts and traditions that may broaden our creative potential to include more beauty and meaning in our own sacred spaces.

One of the ways we can transcend contemporary taboos that trivialize and stereotype beauty and the sacred is to look at the ancient universal symbols and archetypes that still speak to us today. We can import these symbols into our gardens and use them as part of our garden design process, bringing another sacred element into the garden. If we garden with the intention of creating beauty and being more connected with our soul, the garden will respond and evolve according to our own natural flow. We are responding to our soul paths. When we are in tune with the seasons, the life-death-life cycles of nature, then we recognize the ephemeral quality of life. As we see and celebrate life in the microcosm of our gardens, we

can bring wholeness and harmony into our lives. "Wholeness" is not the same as "completion"—it is perceiving the garden or our soul development as a process, not an end product. When we recognize that the garden is always evolving and changing, then we can develop a meaningful, integral relationship between the garden and our ever-evolving selves.

Bringing the wild and the cultivated together into the realm of the garden has been the beginning of my own soul alchemy as an artist—my own rooting as an individual. Being in nature, of course, can put us in touch with the archetype of regeneration, but our own gardens provide us with an intimate relationship of involvement in order to evolve. We are invited to participate in the divine act of ever-growing creativity in a setting where everything is interrelated and self-contained.

The archetypal garden exists in the depths of our imagination. It is about beauty, renewal, and nurture. It can be manifested when we tap into our creativity and get in touch with Nature. We can look to universal symbols, patterns, and shapes that we may want to incorporate in our gardens in order to invest them with more sacred meaning and beauty.

According to Joseph Campbell, archetypes are "elementary ideas" or "ground ideas." Archetypes come from the deep roots of our own unconscious, ancient inutitive source. We can recognize many universal symbols that recur in dreams, art forms, and gardens cross-culturally, which we can choose to weave into the creation of our sacred spaces, like golden threads. Select the threads that seem to have power and energy—perhaps they will begin to appear in your life synchronistically.

ARCHETYPAL ELEMENTS
Golden Threads for
Weaving a Sacred Space

Altar	For receiving offerings and used as a central point in ceremonies and rituals.
Arbor	A canopy of grape leaves for shade, giving us a translucent roof of green-gold living light; also produces fruit of the gods.
Arch	Like a rainbow: from earth to heaven and back to earth. It is the integration of power and love.
Axis	A clear line of sight through which the gardener can look deep within the garden to a focal point inside. In meditation, a clear path from head (ego, control) to heart (soul, the inner path)—the axis of consciousness. In a garden I prefer to deliberately allow the central axis to soften and have an appearance of spontaneous orderly disorder, like Monet's Grande Allée with creeping nasturtiums and no hard boundaries. The axis is the the spine of the garden, the line of site to a focal point, and the path connecting two points as well as leading us through one consciousness into another. (See photo on page 31.)
Bamboo	A sacred plant in most Asian cultures, rich in symbolism. Like the Tree of Life it connects heaven and earth. In great winds it bends but doesn't break, so it

Timber bamboo (Phyllostachys bambus ordes) (above); the Children's Bell Tower, Bodega Bay, California (top right); Bench, Parc des Moutiers, Varengeville, France (lower right)

reminds us to be "rooted, yet flexible," to endure, survive, and conquer adversity. It is also a symbol of graceful aging because it remains evergreen, unchanging with the seasons, and grows more beautiful with maturity.

Bells
Invited to ring by the wind; an awakening reinforcing life dreams, prayers, and visions. The Children's Bell Tower in Bodega Bay, California, was made as a memorial for a young boy murdered in Italy. The boy's parents had donated their son's organs, and the Italians were so touched by their generosity and act of forgiveness that they sent a collection of bells. One has engraved on it the names of the boy who died and the seven people whose lives were saved as a result of the organ donations. The largest bell is from the thousand-year-old papal foundry and was blessed by the Pope. These bells ring spontaneously with the wind, creating a truly sacred space of spiritual inspiration.

Bench
For contemplation; to allow one to sit and be, to experience all the senses in the garden.

Birds
The winged messengers—always depicted in Paradise/Eden, residents in heaven and earth. Aviaries are found in Roman, Chinese, Egyptian, and Aztec gardens. Garden dovecotes are prized in Normandy as status symbols.

Bird feeder	Represents offering of hospitality to the wild.
Blossoms	Ephemeral beauty; a lesson in appreciating the moment.
Bridge	Connecting one side of belief to another; often over and through water (unconsciousness).
Bulbs	Life emerging from dormancy. *See* Lily.
Butterflies	Symbolic of transformation/metamorphosis. Butterflies transform from a lower life form that crawls into a higher, more evolved form that flies.

Cave, grotto	Invites entrance into the womb of the Earth Mother, descent into the dark interior. In rites of initiation, caves and grottoes represented small death, from which one would reemerge into the light of New Life. Caves have been used as earth temples for thousands of years in many cultures, and their walls have held the records of the shamanic journeys and daily life practices of many indigenous peoples.
Circle, cycle	Represents wholeness; has no beginning and no end. The gold ring is used in the marriage ceremony to symbolize eternal love and balance. The earth, moon, and sun are circles, and time—hours, days, years—is measured by cycles of those circles. In the Renaissance, the circle represented a poetic analogy to eternity, heavenly harmony, and perfection. A circle has a center, and it is important in Feng Shui, the Chinese art of placement, to begin in the center—the heart rather than an edge—when creating a sacred space.

A bridge at Japanese gardens in Portland, Oregon (above)

In old fairy tales like "The Handless Maiden," a chalk circle would be drawn around the innocent for protection from evil.

Colors

Depending on one's cultural source, all colors hold various meanings. Choose colors that feel harmonic to you, that complement the light and make your heart sing from the beauty and vibration. This is much more important than every plant being "color-coordinated." Welcome seasonal changes and the effects of light through use of color.

Compost

A pile of organic waste and weeds from the garden, food scraps from the kitchen, and fallen leaves, layered with manure and occasionally turned, which gets moist and dark when allowed to sit still and decompose. Composting is the alchemical process in the garden turning "garbage" into "Gardener's Gold," the richest, best food for the soil to promote healthy growth. When I look at all the weeding and pruning I've done in my own life with people and experiences, I can see that the cast-off layers generate a soul alchemy that promotes my growth.

Enchanted garden

Usually old and with a sense of plants going wild, becoming one with Nature. The enchanted garden evokes a feeling of magic, mystery, and intrigue. In *The Secret Garden* the children felt the enchantment; they were intrigued by the mystery, their privacy, closeness to the little wild animals, discovery, old bulbs coming up, surprise, and a welcome to participate. There was nothing too precious or perfect, like a manicured lawn (not to be walked on!) or controlled shrubs, all clipped whenever they grew.

If we recognize the sacred in Nature we are going to feel the sense of the sacred in a "garden growing wild," not a manicured, heavily controlled space. This also helps us embrace our own authentic "wild natures."

Extended view

Bringing Nature and the world beyond into our private space. Sometimes the most effective view is one glimpsed or peeked at through a hedge, rather than an overwhelming vista that can take us outside our center.

Flower bouquet	Poem from the garden; an assemblage of individual beauty, scent, form, and texture, as a gift from the garden to the gardener and from the gardener to the friend.

Flower fairy mailbox

Often found in old trees; looks like a hole or large crack. This is where children can leave notes and gifts for the flower fairies; if they are lucky and it's an active post, the fairies will remove the notes at night and may even leave messages or small treasures from Nature for the children who believe.

Flowers

Symbolic of femininity, fertility, beauty, ephemerality, impermanence, spiral unfolding, a mandala.

Flowers as offering

Garlands, wreaths, and pyramid-shaped flower arrangements were the earliest designs created by women, made as offerings and decorations for the altars of goddesses.

Fountain

Abundance of life energy; flow of prosperity.
See also Water

Garden

In Christian mythology, the garden is where human life began, the Garden of Eden, home of Adam and Eve. Historically, formal gardens were begun in Sumeria, moving to Greece and Rome, and later throughout Europe, to India via the Moghuls, to Spain by the Moors, and centuries later to the Americas by Spanish explorers and clergy. Some of these examples are seen in the early California missions. I imagine women who used to

Children leave notes for the flower fairies (above); Mission garden with bell tower and statue of St. Francis, Carmel, California (top right); Garden gateway, Brittany, France (lower right)

gather plants for food and medicinal purposes eventually decided to transplant them into a more central location for cultivation, establishing true culture.

Garden house   A shelter from bad weather in the garden. Also, an architectural feature and destination point.

Garland   Traditionally crafted from oak leaves and acorns or laurel leaves; the expression "standing on your laurels" refers to someone honored by being given a laurel garland. Today we mostly use evergreen garlands at Christmas or ones with flowers at weddings. Evergreen garlands are used to decorate mantles and stairways, doorways, fences; places of transition. They were one of the first floral arrangements made by women to decorate the altars of the goddesses.

Gate   Signifies transcendence, departure from one world to the next—wild to cultivated; public to private. An invitation to go deeper, into an inner sanctum—a symbolic death of the familiar to rebirth of a more intimate inner knowledge of self.

There are many kinds of gates, each with a different purpose, style, and meaning. A low, open picket gate is a rather transparent transition compared to a high, solid gate that one cannot see through. Gates with roofs offer protection during transition and are common in Asian gardens. In my own small garden I have four gates, one of which is solid and two that have roofs, and one made of willow.

Gazebo Temple for gods and goddesses; preferably set on high ground for ritual ceremony and protection.

Grassy area For games, play, and gathering, spontaneity and openness. When on the edge of a forest it is known as a place where fairies gather.

Green Man The archetypal male counterpart to the Earth Mother; the son, lover, and guardian of the Great Goddess. He is portrayed as a composite of man and leaf: a great leaf like an acanthus with masculine eyes, nose, and mouth. He is also portrayed as a male face with leaves such as oak or grapevines coming out of his mouth and from between his brows, or his "third eye." The first Green Men were found in Roman sculpture and painting in the first century. The Celts saw him as Esus, the god of Spring, and Cernunnos, the god of the forest, the underworld, and wealth. Like Persephone—the Greek goddess of spring who descends annually to the underworld, creating winter—the Green Man, connected to the ancient forests, makes his descent to the underworld with the roots of the ancient trees. There the true wealth of the soul life can be nurtured.

The image of the Green Man was carved high into the columns of eleventh- and twelfth-century European churches, often placed above statues of Mary, the Great Mother, where he seemed to protect her. The columns are like great trees or totems. Today the Green Man is often portrayed as Bacchus with grapes, appearing on fountains and planters or as decorative masks and salvaged architectural elements.

Archetypally, the Green Man is returning to our consciousness as strongly as the Goddess and the Gaia awareness of Mother Earth as a living being. The Green Man connects us with Nature, as well as our own creative expression and ability to protect the earth from destruction—to heal and call forth the regenerative qualities of spring.

Handmade life	Anything made by hand ourselves, or made by an artist/craftsperson, has soul. The object will contain the spirit of the artist who created it and sometimes the spirit of the natural material it was made from.

Handmade life

Anything made by hand ourselves, or made by an artist/craftsperson, has soul. The object will contain the spirit of the artist who created it and sometimes the spirit of the natural material it was made from.

I recently met a traveling musician who was living partially out of his car and camping at his friend's down the road from me. He had found a place along the river where wild willow grows abundantly. He harvested some green branches and began to bend them into chairs and tables. I'd always wanted handmade garden furniture, so I bought his pieces, and the energy in my garden really changed with the natural chairs and table. I then commissioned him to make some gates for the end of my driveway to keep my little dog in, but with natural openness for seeing beyond. The curving shapes of the gates are like musical sounds; the shadow patterns are delightful. They have beauty and pattern as well as function. I felt like a patron of the arts commissioning this gate, providing meaningful creative work with fair compensation and true appreciation to the artist. Now a whimsical, functional gate with beautiful shadow patterning is in my garden, and I feel the energy of the still-green wild willow and the artist's creative spirit.

Hedge

Living wall, fence; garden enclosure, boundary, division, privacy.

"Hens and Chicks"

(Sempervivum tectorum) A rosette-shaped succulent with tiny baby "chick" offspring that cluster around the mother plant. These waxen, silver-blue plants were used in early California gardens to border raised beds of herbs and were known to keep evil spirits away—always useful!

Herbs

One of the most intriguing, diverse, and useful plant groups. Herb gardens usually fall into one of four traditional categories. *Culinary herb gardens* are planted close to the kitchen door and offer leaves, seeds, bulbs, and blossoms to flavor food. A *physic garden* is made up of medicinal herbs to use as remedies for a multitude of ailments, from headaches to heartbreaks. The *knot garden* is a visual treat: a carefully designed pattern of intersecting shapes interwoven with different colored herbs. The fourth kind is the *Shakespeare garden,* which romantically recalls love sonnets and midsummer night's dreams through its soft textures, colors, and heavenly scents (see page 94).

Icon   A sacred relic, usually a painting, weaving, or bejeweled carving that depicts an image of a holy figure in a symbolic, highly stylized manner. With simple materials a craftsperson can follow prescribed design formats and, with personal, spiritual intention, create a piece of art that becomes sacred. These precious icons become imbued with meaning and sometimes are even associated with miracles through devotee prayer. An icon is a "door to heaven" for sacred communication.

Gardens can become our own personalized icons. If we create them with intention and imbue them with our love and personal meaning, these small patches of land will in turn radiate their own spirit. Some

places on Earth are invested with great spirit, and have been called sacred for thousands of years by indigenous peoples. I believe we can "re-sanctify" the land by putting our own soul and spirit back into it. Any garden space has this potential, just as any person does.

In the icon of the Madonna and Child, painted onto the garden wall of Santa Catalina School in Monterey, California, the blessed Mother Mary has given birth to the Child of Light, who will show us the way to enlightenment, to Paradise on Earth, through love. The Madonna and Child are called icons of loving kindness because they portray the Madonna's motherly love and tenderness for her child. The Madonna is the closest parallel in Christian belief to Mother Earth. Here her baby son looks very adult blessing his mother.

Icon of Loving Kindness, Santa Catalina School, Monterey, California (above)

He represents the wisdom in youth and the child within the adult, recalling the cyclical nature of all life. This Madonna holds a bouquet of wildflowers—offerings of beauty from Nature. Her dress is sky blue and covered with roses, the symbol of love, like the heart in her crown. The mother and child are both supported by the crescent moon (cycles of the feminine), angels, and a garland of pink roses. Together the two figures represent the merging of the earthly, or soul (the mother), with the celestial, or spirit (the child). Symbols from traditional icons can inspire us when we make our own sacred space, combining earth and sky.

Japanese teahouse

A place of serenity carefully located in the garden as a beautiful focal point, as a destination for sacred ceremonies. The teahouse is situated for lovely views of the garden, often near a body of water with a bridge. The architectural elements imbue the concepts of Wabi, Sabi, and Suki: elegant simplicity, patined with age, a graceful extension of Nature. Most teahouses are open to the garden, using no glass as separation.

Traditional teahouses are finely crafted from bamboo and other natural materials, which enables them to be a part of the integral whole of the garden, while they heighten the experience of being in the garden and partaking of the tea ceremony itself.

Labyrinth

Labyrinths have been used for thousands of years and are found among many cultures, including American Indian, African, Celtic, and ancient Greek. Labyrinth patterns have been found painted on cave walls, as well as in Hopi baskets; they are related to the Spiderwoman who weaves the web of life, the interconnection of all. As John Muir said, "Each star is hitched to one another."

These ancient, pre-Christian symbols were incorporated into the architecture of the great cathedrals of Chartres, Rheims, and Amiens, built of stone into the floor. The stone paths could be used for walking meditation. They also symbolize entering into the womb of Mother Earth, or going into the depths of the unknown; of descent and resurrection with new knowledge.

Walking the labyrinth as a sacred tool has been brought back into practice through the vision of Dr. Lauren Artress, canon of Grace Cathedral, San Francisco, author of *Walking a Sacred Path*. Many pilgrims experience the labyrinth as a metaphor for their life's journey.

Labyrinths contain at least seven turns. Sometimes the center that is sought seems farther away or the path seems to be repeating itself, but in actuality the pilgrim is getting closer to the center. Several people can walk the labyrinth at the same time, and it is impossible to get lost or tricked like in a maze because it is flat, a precise pattern on the ground with no walls to obstruct one's view. Labyrinths echo our inner path in that there are no dead ends and you can never get lost; you are always on the right path, which you may walk at any pace. It is noncompetitive, nonjudging, and very centering. (See Mary Holmes's labyrinth, page 98.)

Lantern

Light, guidance. A stone lantern is an important garden element in Japanese gardens and comes in many shapes and sizes for different uses and symbols with specific meanings. For example, there is a special lantern for gazing at the moon in the snow.

Lattice work

Used to obscure views, create shadow play and pattern, create privacy with openness, air, and light. Lattices in Chinese gardens are usually made with tile and have many symbolic meanings, depending on the shapes of the openings.

Light

All of life is dependent on sunlight to grow, and as gardeners we are aware of the specific light requirements of particular plants for growth. We also become aware of the beauty of light effects—backlit leaves with light coming through them and the sparkle of light on dewdrops in the early morning apricot light. For me, light is also a direct reminder of the sacred or divine spirit around us all the time. When the light is especially beautiful I find myself saying "thank you" and feeling such a connection to all of Nature—the light feels like grace.

Lily	Symbolizes purity and the Annunciation; flowers emerge from dormant bulbs. Most incredible are rainlilies, blooming in five days after a storm; crinum lilies bloom only after summer electric storms, when the atmosphere is charged with electrical energy, making nitrogen available in otherwise nutrient-depleted soils.
	The Chinese sacred lily is a type of narcissus with white background petals (purity) and a golden cup (holding sacred knowledge). The Easter lily is a symbol of resurrection, coming back from the dead. Mary often holds a lily for purity and a reminder of the life-death-life cycle.
	The water lily and lotus are born in mud in the dark unconsciousness of water. They rise above to bloom on the water surface, after illumination and warmth have reached to their depths.
Love	Love is as essential to creating a sacred garden space as soil and light. When love is nurtured and allowed to go free we can experience passion—the best fuel for creative fires—and when we know passion, we can join together to really understand compassion—to become attuned to one another, even in suffering. It is so important to cultivate compassion for Earth, for all of Nature, for one another, and for ourselves.
Mandala	A focusing point that centers and opens one's heart. Many flowers open in a spiral from within, as they come into their full bloom. This opening movement is in harmonic order. Our gardens as a whole are centering places, and individual flowers can be used for meditation practice.
	The circle with four parts is also a prayer wheel of the Native Americans and can remind us of the four sacred directions.
	The chalk mandala is a beautiful temporary sacred space, created daily as an offering by Indian women, and is intended to be walked on. It is made with colored chalk in patterns given to each family by the local priest.
Maypole	Symbolically, a Tree of Life associated with pagan fertility rituals in which flower-clad young maidens dance around a pole, interlacing ribbons and

singing songs. Maypole celebrations occur on May Day, May 1 (see photograph of Betty Peck's garden, pages 112 and 113).

Mazes

Mazes are designed to "a-maze" people; to trick or fool them. Traditional mazes are made with solid evergreen shrubs at least six feet high in a geometric pattern that entices one to walk down a path, only to find it's a dead end. Walking a maze, you can't see your destination at the center because of the walls that block your view.

At the famous maze at Hamilton Court in England, hired escorts ensure that frustrated explorers can be led out and not be forever lost inside the boxwood puzzle.

Moon garden

A garden of silver foliage and white flowers, usually night-scented, used for ancient moon worship and romance, and lovely for warm evening celebrations. The moon garden reflects the connection to the tides  and the feminine cycles. Planting with the phases of the moon is an old traditional practice—still advised in the *Farmer's Almanac:* you plant root crops like carrots and beets on the wane, sending energy downward, and above-ground plants on the wax, pulling them upward like the high tide.

Moon gate

A circular opening in a garden wall, typical in Chinese gardens. The moon gate symbolizes transition and cycles (see photograph of the moon gate in the Rockefeller garden, page 80).

Mosaic detail from Lily Yeh's Village of Arts and Humanities, Philadelphia (above); Balinese pyramid-shaped offering (right)

Mosaic	Chips of colored marble, stone, or tile placed next to one another to create intricate patterns and shapes—a very different effect than if the surface were whole and then painted with the same pattern. With a mosaic, like a garden and a life, we lovingly make whole a vision which is unique and more beautiful than an unbroken piece.
Native plants	Unity and harmony with Nature. Native plants from the natural landscape will bring sacred properties into your garden and will teach you about interconnectedness in Nature.
Niche	Goes back in art form to 6000 B.C. It can be seen in Middle Eastern and Mediterranean architecture, as well as kilim carpets. The niche often appeared in a garden wall and symbolized a "view to paradise." When we create our gardens as our own expression of Paradise, we may wish to include a niche. We all inwardly desire to create our own niche, our own view of Paradise.
Obelisk	Symbol of masculine power, of the phallus; manifested in towers, steeples, and pagodas.
Offerings	To feed birds is an offering to the wild. In Bali, daily offerings of flowers and food are placed throughout the garden—especially in gateways for the good and bad gods—blessed with holy water, and presented with a prayer with burning incense to take them to the gods.

Traditionally, Greek women made pyramid-shaped arrangements, garlands, and wreaths for the altars of the goddess. Today, we can see entire processions of Balinese women carrying two- to four-foot-high pyramid-shaped offerings on their heads, carefully balancing them for miles as they walk to temple for blessings.

The Christmas tree itself is basically a pyramid shape decorated with meaningful objects such as angels, stars, and lights. It is like an offering to light up the dark winter season.

Orchard

Stands for our seasonal connection to Eden, food, and coming into fruition—even one fruit tree will connect us.

Paths

Life metaphor of our process and our pace. The material as well as the route, patterns, and elements found along the path all contribute to our experience of the garden and our life path.

Meandering paths—spiral, serpentine—are for going inward, for soul enrichment. Walking or strolling paths are for experiencing more than arrival, as in the Zen stroll gardens for walking meditation. These are usually not laid out in straight, flat, hard surfaces like sidewalks for fast movement, but as stepping stones or loose gravel paths where one's pace will slow down.

Patterns

Patterns, created from pebbles, tile, wood, stone, and brick, can be used in pavements, walks, and walls. Patterns can add beauty, texture, and meaning. Natural patterns such as the silhouette of a bare winter tree against the  sky or a light-and-shadow pattern across a lawn can be considerably more beautiful than the outline of the simple geometric cube shape of a modern building. The infinitely varied patterns in Nature are now closely studied in the emerging field of chaos theory.

Pergola	Long covered walkway with filtered light; protection and connection of one place to the next.
Play	Play sparks creativity and encourages risk-taking. It is important to loosen up and have fun—to be spontaneous. Play helps us accept and even welcome change; it stimulates curiosity ("What will bloom next?"). Play helps us accept that life is about change, process, growth. If we think of ourselves as a stagnant "product," an end result of our life events, then we set ourselves up for crisis—the feeling of inadequacy and not having done enough.
	Lîla is a Sanskrit word that means "divine play," the play of creation, destruction, recreation, and love. It is all of life—living fully in the moment, unattached to the outcome so we can be ever-flowing with creativity.
Pond or Pool	Reflecting pools are conducive to meditation, bringing the sky to ground level, integrating heaven and earth.
Prayer flags	Prayer flags are traditionally used in Tibet to enliven the spirit of a place; to make spirits happy; to attract good spirits in order to favor the local people and watch out for their welfare. The flags blow in the wind to send prayers to the heavens.
	It can be very rewarding and meaningful to make your own prayer flags and hang them in your garden, maybe for a special ceremony like a wedding or the welcoming of a new baby, to offer thanks, or to bless a new home or garden. (See the drawing of Gerald's and my wedding garden on page 136.) They can also seek healing and comfort for someone ill, or safe journey and blessings for a loved one who has passed on. Making flags on cloth with fabric inks can be a way for a family or group of friends to express their feelings creatively and outwardly.
Presence	Presence is fully experiencing the moment. This is our gift, our present, to ourselves, our garden, our friends. This awareness will help us realize and celebrate our sacred space.

Stone patterns, Chinese garden, Vancouver, B.C. (left)

Time in the garden—experiencing the moment, the pause between the breath; fully being in the moment; letting go of fear, stress, and any feeling of incompleteness—links us with eternity. We can then appreciate and celebrate all that we have by being truly present. I felt this with my beloved when he was dying. All we had together was the moment—when I was mourning his illness and depletion or in fear of his death, I missed the celebration of us being together side by side weeding or looking or just being. I had to let go of all fear and stay in love and appreciation to receive the gift of presence.

Rose Symbolizes love, heart opening; given as messages of affection. One use of rose water is to anoint the chakras for healing blessings. Some see the rose as a symbol for each person's soul development: new souls are apt to have a very tight rosebud, whereas a highly evolved person would have a full-blown open rose.

Ruins For showing interconnectedness with the ancient; beauty and respect in the old. Creating "ruins" as a garden folly has been long loved and enjoyed.

Shapes There are five universal shapes: the circle, equidistant cross, spiral, triangle, and square.[1]

Circle: Wholeness, experience of unity

Equidistant cross: Relationship and integration

Spiral: Growth and change

Triangle: Goals, dreams, and visions

Square: Stability and security

Shells, Fossils, Bones These beautiful art pieces and sculptures from Nature can add beauty and energy to our sacred gardens. This is especially true when these objects are hand collected. Then they have a personal connection and each has its own story. In the gardens of old Monterey adobe houses,

[1] *See Angeles Arrien,* Signs of Life: The Five Universal Shapes and How to Use Them. *(Sonoma, Calif.: Arcus Publishing, 1992)*

raised beds are bordered with abalone shells, whale ribs, or old bottles turned neckside down, so the green wells on the bottoms of the bottles catch water. Whale vertebrae are used for pedestals for potted plants.

My garden designer friend Scott Ogden has incorporated his love of shells and fossils in a couple of his Austin, Texas, gardens, using the spiral ammonites shaped like rams' horns in a garden wall and pathways. With hundreds of shells collected from dredge islands, Scott is collaborating with his clients to make a shell grotto. The more personally involved we are—the more stories and memories—the more connection and meanings will be invoked in our gardens.

Shrines   Focal points for artistic expression of a deity, god, goddess, or saint—to bring their blessings and your love of them to your sacred space. Candles, incense, flowers, or other offerings are given at the shrine.

Soil   The earth's mantle that supports all life. The health of our soils is directly connected with the health and well being of all life. Soil and soul are very connected: the deeper, darker, and more fertile the soil or soul is, the healthier and stronger it is—and more growth is possible.

Space   Room to think, to create, to play, to take risks, to make mistakes, and to become fully ourselves. Space is not something to quickly fill, it is more like light—a gift to relish.

Spiral   Ancient symbol for eternity; also the ability to go inward while expanding outward—the essence of many spiritual disciplines such as conscious breathing while doing yoga. The spiral, or labyrinth, has been found in ancient tombs. It implies a death and reentry into the womb of the earth. Death is necessary before the spirit can be reborn. This is the continuous cycle of transformation and purification of the spirit throughout life; the Renaissance alchemists used the word *vitriol* to stand for *Visita interiora terrae rectificando invenies occultum lapidem* (Visit the interior of the earth; through purification you will find the hidden stone). A descent into the underworld such as Persephone's into Hades, which created winter and dormancy, another death, is the theme of most initiation rituals, and is an essential path into our inner souls.

Double spiral: Common in ancient stone carvings in Ireland, the double spiral carved by Megalithic people represents going inward to the small death; going outward to rebirth with light and consciousness.

Spirit house In Balinese tradition, a spirit house for ancestors is carefully situated in the garden according to traditional law, which brings the wisdom of the ancestors into daily focus. Spirit is housed naturally in all gardens.

Staircase Ascension (rising to heavens for a higher level and overall view) or decension (toward the earth, rootedness).

Statue Of gods, goddesses, nymphs, mythological figures, satyrs, saints, animals. Balinese gods provide protection at gates (see Bali photograph, page 72). Buddha is often placed in contemplative settings (see the Rockefeller Garden, page 79).

Saint Francis is the patron saint of the Nature realm and ecology, the Christian counterpart of the pagan "Green Man." Known as a lover of the earth, stars, sun, moon, birds, and other living creatures, he considered

all of God's natural creations part of his congregation. He appears in many gardens today, most often as a small statue. Garden centers often sell a St. Francis statue in a simple triangle-shaped niche, to hang on the wall, sometimes with a bird feeder incorporated into the design. The simple niche symbolizes

A walled garden using arches and a path leading to a statue of the Goddess of Fruit and Hospitality, Château De Canon, Normandy, France (above)

St. Francis leading us to Paradise. (*See* Niche, as well as the photograph of the Mission garden on page 37.)

Stones

Elemental, strong, silent, and long-lasting, stones hold memories of the landscape, complementing the more ephemeral aspects of the garden.

A sacred element in a traditional Chinese garden is the honeycomb-spiraling limestone known as Tai-hu stone, a result of erosion from Tai-hu Lake. The most valued stones are slender with many surface folds, are impermeable to water so they can stay outdoors in the garden, and have a large number of holes. These stones became rare in the Ming Dynasty (1368–1644), and today it is illegal to remove new stones. The Chinese feel a freedom of spirit and a harmony with Nature in their orderly and symbolic gardens.

In Japanese tradition, stones are symbols for mountains. Raked stone gravel in Zen gardens can represent rivers, pools, and waterfalls.

Certain stones—coming in any shape, size, or composition—are attributed with special powers. The Celts placed gigantic, upright stones along the earth's ley-lines (which correspond to the human body's meridians) as specific energy points (like acupuncture points), perhaps for special ceremonies. Celtic women hoping to get pregnant would sleep at the base of standing phallus-shaped stones to improve their fertility. Some people bury crystals in their gardens to improve the energy, and many of us display rocks we've collected from particular places that hold stories and memories.

Sundial

Used since at least 1500 B.C. Functions by direct connection with the movement of the sun and is a reminder of the temporal nature of human life and the passing of time and seasons. Tempus fugit.

Threshold

I like a garden with several thresholds. I prefer to go through a series of gates, walls, hedges, and pergolas, to help me shed the fast public pace and to help me realize and feel a sense of arrival to a sacred inner sanctum.

Each threshold is a crossing over, a marker for going deeper and into more personal space. It is a soul preparation for the visitor as much as it is an invitation or barrier, like a door to a private room. The threshold helps keep our sacred gardens protected, tucked away and private, to be shared by invitation after an initiation.

Totem pole

The Pacific Northwest is richly blessed with rivers, gigantic forests growing to the edge of the sea, inlet waterways, and an abundance of fish and plant life. Because of the generosity of the land, the native Pacific Northwest tribes have had time

to develop their own rich animistic mythologies and art forms. They were so imbued with a true sense of abundance that they celebrated with a potlatch, a feast where there was a giving away of presents. It was during the potlatch that claims of clan and personal animal symbols were made, and totem poles were carved and erected in recognition of these claims. Like family crests, the totem poles told the story of the animistic powers and connections the family had, and in this way gave them status.

Today, the people continue to carve animals such as the bear, whale, or eagle, or combinations

Pacific Northwest totems (top left); Personal totem, Lily Yeh's Village of Arts and Humanities, Philadelphia (lower left)

of animals, birds and fish, which were a personal part of a family's mythology. The carver completely respects the beauty and spirit of the tree he is carving as well as holding the belief that the creatures—power animals—actually exist just on the other side of our visual world. These animals are a source of energy, protection, and insight. It could be a very meaningful process to create your own totem pole, carved in wood or made from other materials—like "Big Man" did in Lily Yeh's Village of Arts and Humanities.

Treehouse Dates back to the first Roman gardens, representing shelter near the heaven in the Tree of Life. Houses in the trunks of trees are more cave-like, more like going into Mother Earth.

Trees Mature trees, the longest lived and largest plant form, carry a beauty and life force all their own. They connect the three worlds: the heavens, the here-and-now, and the underworld. It is extremely important to protect old trees and develop our personal relationships with them. To touch or embrace a tree is to remember all the life force just under the bark.

When we express something positive and then say "knock on wood" and knock on a wooden table, we are recalling an ancient tradition. Back when everyone recognized tree spirits, it would be customary to knock on a tree to awaken the spirits to ask them to reinforce a positive experience or intention.

The ancient Celts used trees growing in rings as "cathedrals," as sites for ritual.

There are many different sacred and symbolic trees. They have many different meanings and associations in different cultures. Here are a few:

Apple: Eden (Tree of Knowledge)

Cypress: long life

Date and Fig trees: fertility

Evergreens: everlasting life; used at winter solstice and Christmas

Flowering cherry and plum: in Japanese tradition, temporality, fleeting beauty

Fruit trees: fruition; changing of the seasons; Eden

Hazel: nuts of knowledge (Fionn gained the Wisdom of the Ages and became the great hero of Ireland after he ingested salmon that had eaten hazelnuts)

Laurel: mythological evergreen used as crown for gods and Olympians

Maple: renewal

Oak: long life, solidity, trust

Olive (branch): peace

Palm tree: Paradise (when near an oasis)

Pine: strength; always alive

Pomegranate: fertility and sustenance; just three seeds kept Persephone alive during her descent to Hades

Trumpet flower: calling up to heaven

Vessels	Symbolic of the feminine—the uterus; source of life.
Walled garden	In all religious traditions God is perceived not only as infinite and all-expanding, but all-encompassing. A walled garden is also a holder of infinite possibilities, offering protection, seclusion, and privacy—an inner sanctum where transformations can take place.
Water	An essential element for all of life. Water is sacred in all cultures with its ability to cleanse, purify, nurture, heal, and grow plants. It represents fluidity and flexibility and connects us to Grandmother Ocean and the water creatures. *See also* Fountain and Pond.
Water basin	Used in Japanese gardens to wash hands and mouth before going into sacred space.
Well	Wellspring—Source that brings forth life, "wellness." ("I hope you feel well soon," we say to those who are ill.) In Celtic lore, the sacred wells

are entrances to the underworld, and in the British Isles are still a place of offerings, ritual, and prayer. Today people put "wishing wells" in their gardens and throw pennies in as token offerings to assure that their wishes come true.

Wildflowers Ephemeral jewels given to us from Nature; a true gift of joy and beauty. I highly encourage walking in wilderness to witness the beauty of wildflower gardens, and then planting wildflower seeds native to your area to create your own small meadow of wildflowers—much better than a manicured lawn. It will also be a lot more engaging and joyful.

Wind chime Drawing music from the wind; a universal, harmonic sound played spontaneously by Nature, bringing positive *ch'i* (energy). When selecting a wind chime for your garden be sure to listen carefully and choose one with a sound that resonates in you.

Wreath Began as leaf and floral circlets for the crown of the head. Traditionally, four open roses were used, placed in the four directions. This was known as a "crowning." Later more precious materials like gold and silver with jewels and pearls were used for making more enduring crowns given to royalty. Garlands are like open wreaths hung around the shoulders and arranged loosely on altars and over doorways. Christmas wreaths are made from evergreens to decorate our front door to welcome guests.

Yin and yang This Eastern symbol represents the darkness which is a part of the light and the light which is in darkness. Like the Tree of Life, each flows into the other to make up the whole. Yin is the magnetic, receptive feminine, and yang is the dynamic, creative male energy.

The Golden Mean

The Golden Mean has been known as the Divine Proportion and called "Golden" since ancient times because it is the perfect division of proportion which is found in Nature, giving proof of conscious evolution and as some believe, the evolution of consciousness as well.

The Golden Mean creates a perfect Unity or Harmony. This radiating proportion has a feeling of expansion which relates back to itself and is contained within itself. Like the spiral pattern in a chambered nautilus shell, each chamber's proportion creates the space for the next one, which creates the spiral. The same proportion is evident in the radiating curves of the seed pattern in a sunflower. This is the same principle by which most cultures perceive God, ever-expanding, but relating back and contained in the whole.

Artists and architects have long been inspired by this perfect proportion in Nature. When art, buildings, and gardens have striking harmony and beauty of form, the Divine Proportion of the Golden Mean usually has been employed.

In the magnificent tenth-to-twelfth-century cathedrals in France, shrines built to honor Mary (many built on sacred Goddess worshiping sites) used principles of divine geometry. The proportions of the Golden Mean were meant to provide worshipers with many experiences of the Divine.

Arches and ceiling height were constructed in such a way that when choirs sang Gregorian chants, their voices rose upward and then echoed downward, like the voices of angels, returning in refrain. The magnificent windows were used to illuminate stories and symbols and cast healing light onto the believers.

An essential quality for enrichment in our gardens and in our lives is harmony and a feeling of centeredness. As gardeners, we create spaces of beauty for retreat, to find quiet, solitude, a place to meditate, maybe as informally as when we weed. The principles for Divine Proportion can also be employed when planning a garden as sacred space.

Essentially, we want to support our souls—to be ever expanding, open and growing. We want each of our life experiences to relate and build on our past, yet move forward on a beautiful harmonic path. When we think of soothing music, we think of a harmonic scale, an interrelated balance of vibrations. Hearing these tones can relax us and put us at ease. It is the same for finding a human proportional scale of space in our gardens, homes, and the places we do our creative work. We desire places where we feel balance and harmony, not ones overpowered by vast looming buildings or surrounded by flat lawns.

As I create a garden I try to integrate my awareness of the principles of the Golden Mean to have a feeling of harmony and balance so that

CULTIVATING SACRED SPACE

when I am in the garden my energies will be renewed and I will have a sense of fulfillment, even when the garden is not complete or "perfect."

I've used the direct Golden Means proportional ratios to design arches, gates, layouts of beds, and paths. I try to have the garden interrelate with the house and the surrounding land or neighborhood. Sometimes we are given gifts of extended views we can invite into our space; more often there are buildings to screen or an inner focal point to create. Each challenge can be transcended when we hold to heart the gifts of the awareness of Divine Proportion and inner connectedness for transformation.

Feng Shui

The Chinese art of placement, Feng Shui is an ancient ecologically based art which strives for complete harmony with Nature. It has been used for centuries in China as well as in Bali to improve people's relationship with Earth's energies, known as ch'i. With positive Feng Shui, one's life can be in balance, and all of one's relationships with family, career, health, and even prosperity can be enhanced.

Some of the practices of Feng Shui are completely common sense and based on ecology and architecture. Other principles are more mystical and employ ritual. Feng Shui can be applied to rooms, cities, and of course, the garden. The art

is immense, and to be a beneficial practitioner requires practice, study, and intuition.

Creating positive ch'i or energy in the garden can be done simply and with intention. The key to Feng Shui is creating a sense of harmony. There are certain elements to consider in the garden in order to create this sense of harmony. It is important to be aware of the light quality and the amount of light in the garden. Including a water element is always beneficial: moving water creates a pleasing sound; a still pond is conducive to reflection. Both produce a calming atmosphere. In Chinese gardens stones with sculptural shapes enhance positive ch'i in the garden (see Stones, page 51). I find using well-placed beautiful stones provides a very "grounding" centerpoint. When landscape architect Rebecca Dye places large rocks in gardens to actually change the energy, the garden owners comment on the positive difference they feel with well-chosen and thoughtfully arranged stones (see Rebecca Dye and Hank Helbush gardens, pages 102–108). Harmonic movement and sound are important elements in Feng Shui. Wind chimes with harmonic tones and ribbons with bells tied from the branches of trees to create more movement and appealing sounds can be integrated into the garden. The natural music of songbirds can be encouraged by attracting birds with feeders, houses, baths, and their favorite trees. Planting flowers and shrubs that attract butterflies also encourages more movement and delightful life forms. Ornamental grasses and bamboo visually translate the graceful dances of the wind. To have a balance of ch'i, it is also important to bring ch'i up into the air and have it move—not have "flat, dead space." We can include flowering trees, climbing vines on trellises, even poles with moving flags that will bring energy up and circulate it like a soft breeze.

Feng Shui can be used to place a building onto an auspicious site and to create positive environments inside structures. Designing homes that are well situated to the land, have good exposure to the sun and protection from severe winds, pleasant views, and a natural extension into surrounding gardens creates positive ch'i. When gardens get more and more natural until they meet the wilds, the land is kept in tact and respected. The soul and spirit is renewed daily.

There are specific ways to restore a sense of balance, when an imbalance exists. For example, if a house sits up above the earth with a high foundation, especially if it rests on stilts and is not solid, this can create an uncomfortable, floating feeling. One possible correction could be to plant evergreen hedges around the foundation perimeter, connecting the house with the ground. If there is direct negative energy coming into a space, like car headlights or traffic noise, an inner wall beautifully decorated might be placed inside the main gateway to deflect the energy and create more privacy and harmony.

(Look at the examples in the Bali gardens, pages 70–72.)

The eight-sided *ba-gua,* which comes from the ancient *I Ching,* is a basic element in the study of Feng Shui. It is situated in a space, not according to the four directions, but to be aligned with the main entrance of the space. In a house that entrance would be the front door, or the most-used door. A space like a garden may have more than one entry, but the ba-gua would be laid down to align with the most commonly used entry. Each corner of the ba-gua corresponds to common life situations, colors, and elements. You can improve specific areas in your life by bringing positive energy to the relative points of the ba-gua.

I incorporated many elements of Feng Shui to encourage positive ch'i when I redesigned and replanted the outdoor gardens of a large local shopping center. My staff and I removed cement in an octagon shape around many cement pillars that were gray, cold, and imposing. After improving the soil, we planted flowering and scented vines to encircle the columns and bring ch'i upward. Then, we planted entire flower beds at the base. This immediately changed the ch'i. Overgrown, dense trees in poor health were pruned and deeply fed, and a few crowded ones were removed to open up views and light.

In a cement courtyard with bright, glaring, reflecting light that made people avoid the area, we removed 3,000 square feet of cement in a softly curving pattern. (This was laid out with long garden hoses, then marked with a thick felt tip pen and spray paint.) A huge mural of a garden looking out to the sea was painted on a neighboring two-story wall, and a flower garden was planted beneath it. We put in a stone path and three rose arches to walk under to encourage children into the garden. We also planted fragrant flowers and plants to attract butterflies and hummingbirds. We installed fountains and more benches for places to sit and rest, many more shade trees, and large potted plants. In three existing raised cement planters, eight jumping life-size dolphin topiaries were placed underplanted with blue flowers and silver grasses. We made a Mediterranean plaza with splashing fountain, tables, chairs, and umbrellas.

I can happily report that everyone from management to shoppers has noticed and appreciated the changes. Everyone's attitudes seem to have greatly improved. Strangers have even thanked me and commented that they like the wild feeling with beautiful colors—it makes them happy. It has been a transformation from an unattractive, utilitarian shopping center to a very enjoyable public garden where people enjoy sitting and being in the space like an old town square, a meeting place.

Vibrations

There are many types of vibrations in a garden, and they bring forth a subtle but profound quality to be aware of—especially when cultivating a sacred space. Most of us have experienced *color vibrations,* most vibrant when two opposite colors like red and green are placed side by side in equal amount and densities. Sometimes there is a wobbling wave feeling (this is a popular technique with op and pop art). We can select and place flower colors next to one another for a vibrational effect.

We can experience *sound vibrations* when we hit a drum and put our hand near the source of its resonance. Once I hit my small round drum with its soft mallet and pointed the drum face toward some crystal glasses I had high on a shelf. The glasses began to sing and resonate. I then really understood the power of sound vibration.

An Aeolian harp can be made in a strong tree, such as an oak. Using eye-hooks screwed into branches of different widths, musical strings can be strung between the branches. Heavy piano strings might be used for a longer distance between heavier branches. Light strings from a violin or a ukulele could be strung on smaller branches closer together. The strings can even be tuned harmonically. The movement of the wind will cause the strings to vibrate, and the sound will be like angels playing harps in the trees.

Plant vibrations are evident in healthy, happy plants. I first noticed this in Princess Sturdza's magnificent garden on the coast of Normandy, France. All her plants are so well placed and so completely loved and well cared for, there is a vibration of health and well-being. But when I have visited Monet's garden on a Sunday afternoon when many people have been there, the flowers appear weary, as if they are tired and worn out with exhaustion. I don't photograph then, I just greet them and wait until they are more rested and refreshed. I noticed a similar and very astonishing phenomenon after the long illness and death of my husband, Gerald Bol. His cherished bamboo, which he had carefully planted over six acres and grown with great devotion, actually seemed to mourn. There was a

Le Vasterival, Princess Sturdza's garden, Normandy, France

visible change in the vibration of the plants. The leaves appeared duller, with less luster and vitality, almost like a plant that requires water just before it wilts. The foreman of the nursery, who also knew the bamboo well, noticed the same thing.

There are many different flower essence remedies that carry *flower vibrations*. The most well known are the Bach flowers, which are from England. These flower essences are used for emotional and spiritual support and are taken as drops in a glass of water or under the tongue. Like homeopathic medicine, these are very subtle yet profound remedies. I have used them for years and have found they help keep me in balance.

Wabi, Sabi, and Suki

We can learn to be aware of the essential Japanese elements of Wabi, Sabi, and Suki so that we recognize, cultivate, and welcome them in our sacred spaces.

Wabi: tranquil simplicity

Sabi: patina of age

Suki: subtle elegance

I first became aware of the Wabi-Sabi-Suki aesthetic—although I had no name for it at the time—through my Grandma Kilkenny's loved and worn treasures which were used and displayed throughout her house. Threadbare, lovingly mended items made by hand were highly valued because of their intrinsic beauty and the stories they told—stories of the country, cultures, the artists, and how the objects came to live with us.

In Japan I again experienced the aesthetic universe of Wabi, Sabi, and Suki and came to value each of the three qualities in objects, places, and people. When I was seventeen, I went to live in a small Japanese village surrounded by rice fields, nestled between the rich cultural cities of Kyoto and Nara. There were no cars, and paths were strewn with chips of blue-and-white pottery. The house walls were made of sand, dung, and split bamboo; the roofs were thatch. My spirit thrived in the tradition and the connections of Nature, Art, Family, and Community. In my Japanese family I loved it that three generations lived in our one house. The living room, which housed the family shrines, became the grandparents' bedroom at night. I loved the hot baths in the evening and the chicken in the courtyard. The singing of the huge temple bell on the hill let us know the time of day. I treasured helping my Japanese mother plant rice in the wet paddies the traditional way. We arranged flowers with elegant simplicity in very old family heirloom vases. It was a centering process, and the arrangements, as focal points, created tranquility.

I came to realize that the Wabi-Sabi-Suki aesthetic is a way of life, a path to follow that respects and echoes Nature in form and function. Using objects in the garden made with natural materials which are allowed to age and weather will create this feel.

Gardening as a way of life, as a spiritual path, provides tranquility and expresses the Wabi concept. When maturity creates beauty with more depth and meaning in an old garden and charm emerges with old trees, moss-covered stone walls, and green terra-cotta pots—this mellowing reflects Sabi. The Suki element in the garden might be the change of light, the way it moves across the space creating shadows or back-lighting leaves, transforming them into stained-glass windows. Suki is seen in the way bamboo and other grasses move in a breeze, in the visit of a hummingbird or butterfly to some of the garden flowers, and in the clouds reflected in a stone water basin.

⊛

There are different ways that people can connect with Nature. Sometimes the connections are rooted in age-old traditions; sometimes they emerge completely freestyle. We are all so different, but we are all creative and resourceful. When we discover what nourishes us and find our voices of expression, we can then truly create sacred space.

SUMMER

I n summer we celebrate the summer solstice, the longest day of the year. Throughout the season, long, hot, bright days promote vigorous growth and expansion. There is much work in the garden just to keep up, and we are thankful for the extra light and increased energy we are given to do it. This is also a time when many people are able to travel and visit other gardens for inspiration. In this season I invite you to visit twelve very different and unique gardens that have touched me. A few are well known and classical; others are very personal expressions in the private worlds of their creators. Each one integrates creativity and Nature with love and personal vision. Each garden invigorates the soul and is rooted in the sacredness of life.

KOKEDERA TEMPLE

Kyoto, Japan

TWELVE GARDENS OF TRANSFORMATION

Kokedera Temple, Kyoto, Japan

CULTIVATING
SACRED SPACE

Kokedera Temple (*kokedera* means "moss") is the popular name for Saihoji Temple. By either name it is the most special garden I have visited in Japan. The Saihoji Temple gardens were begun in the mid-1300s by a wandering Zen priest named Muso Soseki. He had made several earlier, more elaborate gardens and had gained a fine reputation as a garden designer. He made this garden as his final and most-loved work. He created it primarily with great simplicity and reserve, using stones, water, and maple trees. He "planted" the rocks to "grow" and followed the Zen ideals of gracefulness and understatement. The result was very simple and must have felt quite austere compared to what we experience at Kokedera today, but after one hundred or so years, the stones did indeed grow and the moss began to come. The Zen monks who maintained the garden welcomed it.

The real soul of this garden seemed to arrive with the coming of the moss. It feels like the green grace of a benevolent deity. The loving care and consideration that the monks have lavished on the moss over 650 years has been an essential part of their meditation and gives much beauty and gracefulness to their lives.

The moss in Kokedera is the purest example of Wabi, Sabi, and Suki I know of.

Moss is very fragile. It needs pure air; pollution will kill it. It requires a special moist environment with filtered light. It will dry out and even die with too much hot sun and dryness, so it requires just the right tree canopy and all the ponds to help make the right ecosystem. The gardeners must take care to walk upon it softly and not often. They must sweep it with meditative consciousness, using a light, handmade bamboo broom, to prevent leaf fall from becoming too dense and smothering the moss surface. The relationship the monks have with the moss is so loving and respectful. Gardening is a harmonious, sacred act of mutual giving and receiving of beauty and tranquility.

The number of visitors who may come to the sacred moss gardens is limited, due to the impact of too many people on the gardens. Visitors must center themselves in a group meditation before entering. When Gerald and I went to Kokedera, we were asked with the other visitors to take off our shoes before we entered the temple. We then knelt on tatami mats to pray, led by a Zen priest—with chanting, bowing, clapping hands, ringing bells, and burning incense. Then we each sat in front of a small, low desk with a

CULTIVATING
SACRED SPACE

bamboo brush and black Sumi ink and began writing *sutras,* Buddhist prayers, in Japanese characters. After writing for about fifteen or twenty minutes, I thought, "Well, this is fun, now let's go and see the garden." Fortunately, the Japanese woman next to us said, "Oh, no, you must complete writing the sutras and then you may add your own prayer, wish, or intention to put on the altar and the monks will pray for you, too." This was lovely, so for an hour Gerald and I wrote these sutras; we were, of course, the last people to leave the temple. Before we did leave, we gave

all our Japanese writings to the Zen priest, who looked them over, bowed to us, and motioned for us to put them on the shrine. Then we were allowed into the garden.

This calming experience of focusing on the sutras prepared us to let go of the city and get into a tranquil, meditative place, so that when we passed through the garden gates, we were able to leave behind the fast-moving pace of the world. We entered a new world of tranquility and softness—the true meaning of patina of age. I couldn't help but wonder what it would be like if Monet's garden required visitors to center themselves—or if I did myself before entering my own garden.

Another aspect of visiting a sacred Japanese garden that is very important is the purification ritual. You take a bamboo dipper and dip it in the water that's usually kept in a stone trough or a big round stone with a bowl carved in it, then with the dipper you wash your hands and sometimes your mouth. It's a very graceful way, mentally and physically, of preparing yourself to enter the garden—a respectful cleansing as well as a blessing, like dipping fingers in holy water at a Christian church or in the holy wells in the British Isles. You leave something behind to enter into another realm.

What we see today when we visit Kokedera is truly a moss temple. One of the parts of the garden I really love is the gateway, where we left the very natural garden to enter an even wilder place where the wild timber bamboo forest grows. You must cross over a granite stone bridge over a waterway, then enter an open gate with a prayer on it and a tile roof. Then you ascend, go upstairs, into the woods. There is a meditation

CULTIVATING
SACRED SPACE

platform in the woods, which was the cherished place of the garden maker hundreds of years ago.

Kokedera is designed as a stroll garden for meditation. When you walk along the meandering pathways you see different perspectives and you are offered different kinds of reflections. There are many bridges that are completely moss-covered, and so are never walked on by visitors, but they are there to connect different parts of the space, such as an island (like an individual) to another part of the land (as part of the integrated whole). Beautiful Japanese maple trees make

graceful canopies overhead. We were there in the summer, and luckily there had been a lot of rain, so the moss was very happy and very alive and vibrant. I'm sure that in autumn with the red leaves, in spring with plum blossoms, or in winter with a dusting of snow there would be different visual delights and insights—imagine the patterns of red leaves, pink petals, or white crystals on the green moss.

This garden was my favorite in Japan because of its closeness to and respect for Nature. The natural beauty has been lovingly cared for. In the ponds and waterways that you walk around sits a lovely little boat, and I'm sure that the monks use it when they clean the water. The caretakers of Monet's gardens use a similar boat when they rake the algae off the pond. At Kokedera there are even stone islands out in the middle of the water, where small, naturally bonsaied maple trees grow happily.

When this garden was made it was not graded; the movement of the land itself was respected and nurtured, which is not the common practice today. Over so many hundreds of years I'm sure Kokedera has grown and changed bit by bit. It's a wonderful combination of having a design and an idea, giving loving, skilled maintenance to the gardens, and also welcoming Nature to come forward. The moss is a gift from Nature, and now there are about one hundred varieties of moss that grow everywhere. I know of some gardeners who have used chemicals to keep moss out of their gardens so as to have a "perfect lawn"—what a shame that would be here if the original idea of an austere rock garden had been rigidly kept and the moss killed. But now, how inspiring it is to have the sacred intention of the Moss Temple evolve with Nature.

Balinese Garden

The Balinese have a unique kind of Hinduism that is a little different from that practiced in India. Bali Hinduism is infused with the island's rich, dynamic offerings of Nature, which are intricately interwoven into the fabric of daily life. There is a symbiosis, with balance creating harmony, beauty, and sacredness in the everyday. Time is valued differently. Time does not mean money, as it does for most Westerners. Time is first of all for devoting to family life, for helping at the temples in the many involved ceremonies, and for preparing daily offerings. Creative work like painting, carving, and jewelry making are usually done at home, often with a small group of friends sitting on mats, talking and working together. Collaboration and community are strongly valued, as are taking care of family and village.

The Balinese people are an inspiration for the world in the way they have so lovingly and courageously preserved their very rich and beautiful culture. Bali Hinduism is pantheistic: gods are a part of the entire universe. Spirits are acknowledged in great trees; good gods and bad gods are honored daily with offerings (as the Balinese want to keep both happy); the dark and light side of people's natures and the ways of karma are recognized. The Balinese way of life is a harmonic blend of living in Nature, in their

CULTIVATING
SACRED SPACE

spiritual life, and expressing themselves creatively. There are no words for "artist," because everyone is an artist; there is no word or concept for "private" because the river and the beach are for everyone. When Westerners buy land and put up signs like "Private Land—No Trespassing," the Balinese have no idea what that means and understandably cannot conceive that their ancestral washing place is now not communal.

The Balinese take ideas, designs, or philosophies they admire from other cultures and quickly and easily adapt them into their own way of life. When the Chinese occupied Bali, it was a painful time for the Balinese, but they took some of the positive things from the Chinese such as some elements of architecture and a Balinese version of Feng Shui, and designed them into their lives. The best example is the entrance to the home compound, which consists of a series of separate open-sided, roofed platform rooms used for different purposes, like food preparation and eating, sleeping, and bathing. The placement of the ancestor spirit houses as well as where the pigs and chickens should be are all prescribed according to what results in the most positive ch'i and harmony. All are surrounded and connected by gardens, sometimes with a fountain and small pool with water lilies.

The entire garden compound is raised above street level and walled in. A large roofed gate, usually ornately decorated and often with big statues of gods looking very fierce and frightening, guards the entrance. To enter, one must walk up steps and cross a very impressive, beautiful but imposing threshold, carved with great detail. Immediately there is another wall, again very beautiful and usually with a small, more benevolent god. One must walk around the wall to actually enter the home garden. This inner wall provides the family with much more privacy and is a typical Feng Shui "correction," to keep direct ch'i from blasting into the house from the street. It works.

Because everything is open and there are no locks on the doors, the process of first ascending stairs and then crossing great thresholds through guarding gods is so impressive that one must be very intentional about entering the space. It also clearly distinguishes private space from public. Loud, busy cars can be bustling outside the garden wall while inside it is completely tranquil, full of peace and harmony. In the center of the garden, light shines down, and it is like a direct portal to heaven.

Each day offerings to the gods are placed at doorways, paths, and any possible meeting places of gods. The most common offerings are held in small, carefully woven baskets of palm fronds with flower blossoms such as bright pink bougainvillea and rich golden marigolds, along with a little bit of rice and banana slices. These are placed down in the early morning with a

CULTIVATING
SACRED SPACE

prayer. When the prayer is being uttered, a flower that has been dipped into holy water from a sacred spring is held between the fingers. This water is sprinkled on the offering. A stick of incense is lit to take the intentions up to the gods. These are placed in the family spirit houses in the garden to remember the ancestors' spirits as well.

On holy days, three-foot-high pyramid-shaped offerings of flowers, fruit, and sometimes even rice and duck are artfully arranged and carried on the heads of women for miles to their temple for blessings. Small daily offerings will litter sidewalks in the cultural center of Ubud, which are swept up at the end of each day. Altars will be erected in unpredictable places such as forests and rice paddies, and on busy street corners. Offerings will even be found on dashboards of taxi cabs and tied on to motor scooters to ensure safe travel.

The sacred temples are open to the sky. Highly decorated umbrellas are used over statues, shrines, and altars as symbols of protection and to bring the ch'i up and around the sacred place. Skirts of black-and-white checkered cloth are wrapped around statues, representing the

dark and light, good and bad, life and death cycles of life—like the yin-yang symbol. The huge ficus trees with their immense aerial roots are considered a sacred place, and black-and-white checkered cloth is wrapped around their trunks as well. When somebody passes by in a car they beep the car horn in respect to the spirits that live in these big trees.

Whereas Japan has all the restraint and all the elegance of simplicity, Bali is, in a way, the opposite. Bali is exuberant with vibrancy and cel-ebration and color and spontaneous movement. In Bali there is music, dance, and abundance;

everything has meaning and is part of daily ritual and spirituality. Foreign visitors are welcome to attend sacred rituals as long as they follow and respect local custom and dress. The hospitality of the Balinese opens the hearts and souls of many culturally and spiritually hungry travelers. The Balinese have a very clear intention to preserve their culture, their magic, by practicing it every day. They get nourished by all their art and beauty and ceremonies, so they have the power and energy to protect it. Everything is open because the spirit that is being honored is in all things, in all people, in all plants—in all of the beauty of

Nature. That's why I feel so much at home there. In both the Moss Temple and in Bali the spirit of place must continue to be protected—the delicate moss, as much as the delicate balance in Bali in keeping the rich, traditional ways—from the encroaching modernism that can bring air pollution and heavy feet treading on the fragile moss.

The Abby Aldrich Rockefeller Garden, Seal Harbor, Maine

In America, we have the opportunity to combine what we have learned and loved from many cultures into our diverse natural landscape. The garden of Abby Aldrich Rockefeller in Maine is a wonderful example of this. In 1926 she worked with the great woman landscape designer of the time, Beatrix Ferrand, and together they created a garden that has much sacred meaning and symbolism from Asia and Europe. It is a most remarkable garden because of its grand collaboration of visions, spiritual philosophies, and Nature—designed, most importantly, with great respect for the natural landscape surrounding it.

In 1910, John and Abby Rockefeller purchased a house sitting atop granite bluffs surrounded with woodlands and island views in Seal Harbor, Maine. This area is naturally rich with luscious mosses, lichen, granite, rivers, lakes, white paper birch trees, and the sweet-smelling balsam fir that mingles with the salty sea air. I was eighteen when I first left home in California to garden with Helen and Scott Nearing on this coast. I also fell in love with this land of granite islands and fir trees. This is where I return annually to renew my soul.

In 1921 Abby and John took an extensive trip to the Orient, going to mainland China to commemorate the opening of the first Western medical school there. They were both very interested in Asian art, and John already had acquired an extensive collection of it. As with all deeply cultural art forms, seeing it in the context of the place, people, and traditions in which it was conceived gives the art a profound soul context.

The Rockefellers were invited to the Forbidden City complex in Beijing, where they went to the more private Imperial Rest Garden, with its curving rosy walls capped with golden glazed tiles similar in design and scale to the wall they later were to build in their own garden. They also went to see the intimate gardens at the Temple of Heaven—an auspicious name to receive inspiration for their own garden. Graceful curving walls protected the garden from the outside world and embraced Nature within, rather than keeping it out as in many Western models. The main entrance gates were impressive and meaningful thresholds and usually framed a parallel path to the west.

They traveled for nearly four months in

Korea, China, the Philippines, and Hong Kong. They purchased seven pairs of Korean stone statues over six feet tall. On their return they puzzled on how to blend the beauty of the natural woodlands with the Chinese sensibilities they were so touched by—and with a flower garden. Abby, a great lover of beauty, color, and flowers, had also envisioned a large cutting garden where flowers for fifty arrangements could be cut, and still the garden would be abundant with flowers.

Beatrix Farrand was a highly acclaimed landscape garden designer—with extensive training as a botanist with native plants—as well as a fine artist and skilled architect. She had traveled extensively in Europe, where she met Gertrude Jekyll, the great English garden artist, the master of color rhythms in perennial borders. Beatrix had completed ten years of work on a Chinese-style garden nearby in Maine. She was commissioned by the Rockefellers in the autumn of 1926, which marked the beginning of a collaboration that lasted over ten years for the making of this sacred garden.

When a garden designer is engaged today, it is usually only for devising a plan and possibly the initial installation of the plants and architectural elements. This instant approach to garden-making doesn't allow for a true relationship of client, designer, and place, which must mature over time.

Since this garden's original conception, there was to be a sculpture garden and an extensive flower-cutting garden side by side, though kept visually separated by a wall. It was situated away from the original house and reached by a woodland path. It was never designed to be an extension of the house like a garden room, but a distinct and secluded destination. The initial visual separation of the philosophically different flower garden and woodland sculpture garden was united with a strong axial relationship. The rosy brick wall which embraces the entire garden was built three years after the project began when the Rockefellers were informed that some golden glazed roofing tiles were going to be available from the Imperial Palace in Beijing. This provided an essential detail enabling them to make a wall similar to that in the Temple of Heaven and the Imperial Rest Gardens. The curving mason wall provides the strongest Chinese element, as it holds the two distinct gardens separately, yet as a whole. The rose and gold colors radiate warmth, especially in contrast to the cool, misty climate of coastal woodland Maine.

My favorite gate in the Rockefeller garden is the main south gate. It reminds me very much of Kokedera, the Moss Temple, but the tile roof is bigger and more formal, with cut stone steps and two seventeenth-century stone ram statues from Korea on either side of the gate. This gate frames the woodland Spirit Path into the gardens and, upon leaving, the wild woods with a stone lantern, which lights a path into the woods leading to the house.

CULTIVATING
SACRED SPACE

The spirit path was laid out according to the Imperial tomb design tradition on a north-south axis. The seven pairs of stone guardians, each over six feet tall, line the walk. The prime Oriental intention of simplicity and refuge in Nature is strongly established with the use of entirely indigenous plants, such as native blueberries, bunchberry, wintergreen, mosses, cranberries, and fern. These were planted in masses in a naturalistic manner that softens the path and distinguishes the sculptures. Maple and birch trees were planted for year-round interest, and

light and shadow play, as well as adding strength and power to the processional path.

Beautiful statuary and lanterns brought from Korea, China, and Japan became accents and symbols of great beauty in the garden. A small reflection pond is situated in the woods and made from the gorgeous granite found there. There is a small, simple bench to sit on for reflection and meditation. The pathways are made with large slabs of local granite.

The most striking element I saw in this garden was a beautiful golden Buddha sitting on a

CULTIVATING
SACRED SPACE

huge lotus blossom, placed on a large granite slab in the woods, with irregular pieces of granite leading up to it and the roots of the forest all around with moss softening the crevices. I've never seen any statue more beautifully placed, and it was a complete surprise for me to come across it. Were we to sit under trees like this statue—and, indeed, like Buddha did in his quest for enlightenment—and breathe and watch the trees breathe, our minds would surely be enriched and our spirits and souls would grow.

All color from the sun-drenched flower garden inside the rosy walls was screened from view. Mrs. Rockefeller's favorite entrance to her flower garden was through the "vase gate," named for its fitting shape. In Chinese gardens it is also known as a peace gate because the words for "vase" and "peace" have the same sound.

Within the wall dividing the flower garden from the woodland is a beautiful, soft pink moongate. The moongate is a framework for a second gold Buddha in a woodland setting as well as an entrance to the sunny flower garden—completely different feelings—like the yin and yang, shade and sun, natural and ornamental, one into the other.

Mrs. Rockefeller and Mrs. Farrand collaborated to make a flower garden at first for both display and cutting, in the tradition of Gertrude Jekyll, with living tapestries of color, line, and texture. During this evolution they tried out and grew close to sixteen hundred species of annuals and perennials, including ornamental grasses. Later the garden was simplified, and a master list of more than six hundred plants was developed, including wildflowers to be used in the borders as display only.

Abby Aldrich Rockefeller's garden is an art form that has evolved through time; fortunately it has been conserved and lovingly cared for. It grows as an inspirational example of blending Eastern and Western philosophies, natural and ornamental environments, and embracing different visions to create a sum greater than its parts. It is a testament to the nourishment she got from her travels and her gardens. Now I hope it may continue to grow for another six hundred years, so that it truly takes root.

Monet's Water Lily Garden, Giverny, France

M ost people who are familiar with Claude Monet's paintings know about his great passion for light, beautiful flowers, and his water lily garden. He lived for the second half of his life in the small village of Giverny, where he created a flower garden, a home, and a studio. Surrounded with all this beauty and light, Monet's new paintings sold incredibly well and he had financial stability for the first time in his life. When he heard the village intended to make a starch factory across the street from his flower gardens, he got together the money to buy the land. He then decided to dig a pond, divert the little creek that went through the land to feed it, and grow water lilies, a whole new kind of gardening for him.

It took a couple of years and a lot of frustration, but he kept his vision clear, and when the pond began to mature and his water lilies grew, Monet realized that the pond caught the light in a most enchanting manner. It was his flowering mirror. When he studied his pond, Monet saw how the ever-changing light and patterns of the sky and the clouds and landscape reflected in the water. It was everything that he had searched for. He painted it over and over again, always pushing himself to paint the fleeting light. Monet was the first Western artist to paint a landscape without a horizon line, where the clouds and sky appear abstractly between floating flowers amid the water.

I agree with those who have referred to Monet as a pantheistic priest. He experienced the sublime in Nature, and then magically painted it on his canvases. His true appreciation of Nature attained a certain purity. Nature in turn responded to Monet—there was a sacred connection. Central to this connection was actually making the garden and then being out there—a part of all the elements, soaking up the experience—in the presence of so much life and light. This is like the Chinese cosmology in which the earth spirits secrete moisture and the heavenly spirits secrete light. At the pond both were happening, yet there was a stillness and simplicity in the tranquility of the water where the light could fill his eyes and his soul. It was a place of serenity and renewal for him, a place where he could heal himself. He had a period of great depression when his second wife, Alice, died in 1911, followed by his son Jean in 1914. Many of his dear old friends, like Renoir—people who understood him—died also, and then there was the

devastation of World War I. During these periods of mourning, Monet went to his water garden and watched the light. With the renewal of the day, his spirit would begin to be renewed.

In his late seventies and early eighties, Monet got a very strong inspiration to be able to provide this calming beauty as a gift to all of his countrymen, to all of the war-ravished Frenchmen that he dearly loved, to be able to give them the gift of tranquility that he felt when he was by his pond. He decided to create two oval-shaped rooms in which people could walk into the middle, look around, and see the effect of the changing light that Monet had actually experienced, internalized, and painted with such great passion. He felt that by experiencing the changing light and the beauty and renewal, their souls would be renewed and they would be able to grow and heal as he had healed.

This was a huge endeavor that required all his effort. Today at the l'Orangerie museum in the Tuilleries garden in Paris, you can go down to the basement into the two oval rooms that were built according to Monet's specifications. There his canvas paintings are actually adhered to the curved walls. You can sit in the middle and look around and be touched by the beauty he created. He referred to these paintings as his "bouquet to France." In the first room there are large, contrasting areas of dark drama with firelight coming through. One actually experiences the light and the dance of the water lily blossoms across the pink clouds. In the second oval room all is blue and very calm. Close up the paintings are more like tapestries with many layers. The water lilies are teal and lime green with dark violet and moss green. They float atop soft mauve and lavender with darker blues applied on top, with the mauve still showing through. The willow tree trunks are deep purple with violet and bits of orange. The brush strokes for the water are mostly horizontal; for the lily pads, circular; and for the willows, broken and curved. Monet devised his own form of calligraphy, color relationships, and brush technique to translate and convey what he saw and felt in the presence of this great light. The enormous, full-size canvases convey much power and movement.

Another important design element and symbolic element in Monet's water garden is his bridge. This curved, humpbacked bridge that we

know so well from his paintings was inspired by one of the Japanese woodblock prints he owned. For the first couple of years the bridge was without a trellis on top; he added one later along with both white and lavender wisteria to grow upon it. This way he would have even more softness on the bridge and more reflections to paint. The bridge actually continues the axis of Monet's gardens: if you started at his front door and walked down the Grand Allée, that great tunnel-like walk covered with nasturtiums and the trellis of roses over it, you'd go through the gate, cross the road, pass through another gate, and there you'd be at the foot of his bridge. This is how he liked to take his visitors through his garden. Then you would cross over the bridge and come to a small island on the other side, where he had planted a bamboo garden, another Japanese symbol of connecting heaven and earth. This bamboo probably came from the old nursery in Anduze in the south of France, the Bambouserie, which is still open to visitors and still very viable.

On Monet's pond, no matter what the time of day, the light changes very quickly. At dawn there is a golden light. If it's misty, it's a sparkling shroud of silver and diamonds. It's so lovely. In the moonlight it's lit with another kind of silver that illuminates and reflects. Early in spring all kinds of cascading cherry blossoms and blooming azaleas and wisteria are reflected. The pond has a different feeling and fewer flowers than the flower garden; its simplicity makes it a more tranquil and reflective place, with a smell of moist greenery.

Esalen Institute Meditation Gardens, Big Sur, California

Another garden that I really love, and where I go for soul renewal, is the Esalen Institute. This spectacular place is right on the cliffs of the Pacific Ocean in an area the Esselen Indians always recognized as a sacred place. It is blessed with natural hot springs that come out of the rocks, where one can take healing and rejuvenating baths overlooking the breathtaking cliffs to the ocean, with dolphins and sea otters playing below. There are twenty-seven acres, natural and landscaped, with a large organic garden full of flowers, vegetables, and herbs, which grow year-round to feed the visitors. Esalen is an educational retreat center, and for the last thirty-five years it has brought together philosophers, psychologists, artists, and religious thinkers, blending Eastern and Western philosophies, helping to expand human capacities.

I love to sit on one of the benches by the small Buddha and look across the vegetable garden to the ocean. A lovely curved post with wind chimes above it has been built next to the bench as a small focal point. Like in Bali, people come and bring flowers and place them on the Buddha on an informal, daily basis.

One of the happy, playful elements in the vegetable garden, is a big red goddess with her arms outstretched, just blessing the garden. One of my treasured images of Esalen is of her looking right up into the face of an eight-foot sunflower growing beside her.

My favorite place is a rock ledge where a gushing river meets the sea. Here, it is believed, the Esselen Indians performed their sacred sweat rituals for purification. Now visitors can use a small redwood roundhouse for meditation. There is a wild, rushing sound and a hand-written sign in Japanese and English that says, "Tao follows the way of the water course as the heart mind through meditation returns to the sea." The sign also has a yin-yang symbol. When you walk past the roundhouse to a precious, small garden, right where the river is rushing by you, you have a view to the sea just a few yards ahead. Adding to the uniqueness of this sacred space is a big black-and-green bronze cauldron called a "ting," with a yin-

yang sign on the bottom. It is always filled to the top with water, and always running over a bit. You feel completely integrated with Nature. Plants flourish all about you as you witness this return to the sea—the source of all life. This is a place of repose as well as a place to restore one's vitality—a place to experience Nature and embrace life as you come to understand the full potential in your own self.

As you walk along the path you notice it is full of wonderful hand-collected rocks and shells—big pink rose quartz, coral, and other magical stones, loved by people from all over the world who have sent them in memory of Dick Price, the founder of Esalen who was killed by a falling boulder in 1985. So this is a memorial garden as well as a centering garden where great energies converge—the river, the sea, rocks, and a portal opening to the sky. It is a coming together of some of the great energies and the five elements of air, water, earth, wood, and metal. For many people Esalen is recognized as

88

CULTIVATING
SACRED SPACE

an important power spot on the West Coast, like a beacon or a portal. It is a place where people from all over the world come for healing and transformation. The Esselen Indians recognized it as a window to heaven and painted healing hands on a nearby rock cliff.

Mark Brown's Personal Gardens of Tranquility, Varengeville, France

Mark Brown, an extraordinary garden artist and dear friend, lives in a sixteenth-century walled garden in Varengeville, on the Normandy coast of France. Here he has created seven different gardens, each with a completely different inspirational source, plant palette, fragrance, and feeling. His most personal garden is a verdant "moving garden" of various shades and

forms of green foliage and luminous white flowers. Each plant originates from Japan. He derives
inspiration not from the formal Zen rock gardens
or temple moss gardens, but from Japan's wild
woodlands. Upon pushing open the old wooden
door in the solid stone wall and entering the garden, an utter transition of worlds occurs.

You leave behind the bustle; there's even a
modern housing development that's being built
across the street and the butcher shop is next
door with big carcasses hanging—and Mark is a
strict microbiotic vegetarian. Yet, with all this

going on so closely, there is such stillness in
Mark's garden. One enters into an ethereal, wild,
and sacred place, a private dream world dedicated to contemplation. The scent is a complex
blend of woodsy, damp, sweet greens and a tree
that gives elusive fragrance from its leaves when
the sun warms it, but not when you touch it. You
can only glimpse his stone house through the
lush planting of ten-foot-high grasses and flowering trees, vines, and shrubs. There is an extraordinary spiritual feeling of peace and freshness.
The effects of light and rain completely transform

this garden. It is a "moving" garden because not only do the grasses move in the breeze, but they are allowed to reseed and establish themselves where they are happiest and feel the most at home. Mark allows them to move around in this free-spirited way.

When you get to his front door, there is a little courtyard of stones that he has either collected from the beach and hand-carried (because he doesn't drive) or he has found in the fields as pieces of cut stone and broken pieces of chalk rock. There are big pots of coltsfoot *(petisite japon-ica),* with the wonderful round leaves that you also see along the pond in Monet's garden, and a place to sit and drink a cup of tea and look at the garden—a real meditative spot. Whenever I go, even in the late autumn or winter when the leaves turn golden and things begin to freeze or change shape or form, I feel welcomed by the garden. In the wind and the rain it glistens and changes and I always feel quite at home there.

When I go to visit I often stay in his garden house, an immensely calming place. A couple of years ago, I traveled there with my niece, Rebecca,

CULTIVATING
SACRED SPACE

when she was just three years old. She had jet lag and was exhausted and had been crying and crying. She's a remarkable child, really special, but it was so dreadful for her. She seemed inconsolable. I didn't want to bring her to Mark's quiet sanctuary garden being the way she was—totally out of control. But when she arrived there she just fell under a spell; she completely changed—Mark's gentle, humorous way, his little cat, and the whole environment was so calming. It is just like going to a different land when you go to his garden. It's the original land; it's like how things used to be.

People remember—that's why it's so powerful. We remember this simplicity, this ease, this presence of Nature. This is home. It's what we all are capable of doing and feeling.

On the other side of his home, at his back door, there is much more sun exposure; it is much drier and the plants he has grown there are all in colors of bronze and sulfur yellow and silver moonlight. There are light catchers in the grasses that glow and shimmer. He doesn't try to keep the garden within tight boundaries. The plants that are happy to grow in chalk rock creep

forward and add a texture and a soft edge like an old Persian carpet beginning to unravel.

The garden in front of his house on the sun-drenched side is a charming herb garden composed of a series of patchwork squares, which proceed down a main axis. Each block is an exquisite tapestry filled with incredible textures, scents, and patterns, all in different shades of pink, lavender, silver, and acid greens. Mark has chosen these herbs according to the plants that Shakespeare mentions in his sonnets. So this garden, too, has a very special feeling to it, and, of course, it is a very busy place. Here you can always see bees humming and butterflies landing and his little cats playing. The tapestry herb garden is fun to walk through, touch and smell, as well as to view from above, perhaps on a ladder, looking at all the different textures like a bird.

Mark has a real fusion with Nature. He isn't set in a particular spiritual tradition, but the garden is his whole way of life; it is the whole art, the whole creation, the entire environment, his full expression. He has absolute loyalty to his vision. It's funny, but he told me he doesn't believe in Nature spirits—yet he is so connected. He's more connected than anyone I know. But I don't think that the Nature spirits care that Mark doesn't see them, because they're hanging out in his gardens anyway!

Mary Holmes's Gardens, Santa Cruz, California

Mary Holmes is an artist who is now eighty-seven years old and still very much creating her own visions. She is intensely "racing death," as she says, to complete a major work before she dies. It is a huge icon piece made out of five-foot hinged panels of plywood. The outside doors illustrate the dark side of love and femininity, and then they open as an expansion of the illuminated epiphany of love and beauty. Behind these panels is an inner box with many goddess statues.

For over fifty years Mary taught art at the university level, and since 1969 she has lived up a steep and rutted mountain road with seven major switchback turns (which for her symbolize the seven stages of life), way up in the Santa Cruz mountains near the central coast of California. This is where she can keep all of her beloved animals—her seven horses that run free in the hillside, her many sheep and peacocks, chickens and dogs—companions that enrich her life. Here she continues to paint her visions. She paints her mythology, her archetypes, her gods and goddesses. She has created buildings for them—chapels dedicated to the Mother of us all, and to the Holy Spirit that she sees and feels in all living things. Her work is a process of continuing creation. She does not limit herself by perfectionism or in what she might complete or not complete. She continues to make things and to have a vision.

For me, painting is a focusing. The main thing is a loss of self. It isn't any good if you don't lose yourself. I think the most mysterious thing about us as human beings is that the only time that we experience greatness is when we lose ourselves. Everyone knows it—if you go to a concert you might say, "It wasn't any good; I couldn't lose myself." It's the same thing if you read a book or go to an art exhibit or dance. You have to do it in order to make anything and in order to enjoy anything. It doesn't matter what it is. It's the experience of being transported out of yourself into something larger than you are.

When you experience work coming right through you—while you lecture, paint or anytime you create—that's Holy Spirit. It's extremely mysterious and is experienced by people who are trying to make something. They know the difference when it comes through them and when it doesn't.

It's a lot about readiness and trust. I always like to point out to people that a gift is something that can't be earned and can't be bought or manipulated. Sometimes it's very hard to accept a gift because a gift has a quality of binding. It's also about all the things I've been painting here: compassionate love, temperance, fortitude, Eros, faith, hope, self control—all things people may want but not be able to receive. In our terrible and peculiar times it's difficult for

people to see love. It's one of the things we suffer from—not having the trust to really love.

In Mary's garden there are many chapels: the Sophia chapel, the Wisdom chapel, the Virgin Mary chapel, and the largest center chapel dedicated to the Holy Spirit—actually the whole garden is dedicated to the Absolute Spirit, the giver of life, which is neither masculine nor feminine. One of the very unexpected small chapels purposely looks like a gardener's toolshed on the outside. Inside the door is a jewel box painted black and decorated with golden flowers and birds made from brass that Mary found in secondhand stores. Then there's her statue of the Mother of us all, with an exposed breast ready to feed the world and an apron full of all the animals in the animal kingdom. Mary has a great sense of humor, along with her well-grounded and hardworking spirit, and when she brought me inside we both burst into laughter because it was such a surprise—so fun and unexpected. She has filled this little teahouse temple full of all different kinds of stuffed animals people have given her.

Another wonderful element in Mary's ever-evolving garden is her labyrinth.

I'd always wanted a labyrinth, but I didn't know why or where to put it. There was this

CULTIVATING
SACRED SPACE

extraordinary greatness because my friend knew this woman, Lauren Artress, who was at Esalen in Big Sur right then, giving a workshop on labyrinths, and she came by. I told her I wanted my labyrinth to have seven turns and be based on Chartres. She said it must be twenty feet square and should have a path at least eighteen inches wide with two inches between. Then I went to my wonderful work-man Larry and I said, "I want you to make me a labyrinth," and he said, "What is it?" I showed him a picture. He made a compass with a board and nail and string. He drew it in the

ground and then put forms on it. The most mysterious thing is no one knows why anyone ever made a labyrinth—no idea—and yet it's the only form that has been made all through time. There's no place that's never made a labyrinth—and there's no time—even on cave walls, so obviously it wasn't always to walk. Literally no one knows. I thought, mine has seven turns so I'll make it in the image of the creation of the world. So when you walk my labyrinth you walk through creation, through Paradise. It's intended to remind you of the Divine origin.

Many people think of walking the labyrinth as a way to balance themselves. Mary—because she has her balance with her art and her nature and her animals and her life of creation—feels that her labyrinth is about inspiring people to create. On the concrete walls in her garden, house, and studio, she has made whimsical stained-glass windows: not the fussy, carefully measured and cut geometric shapes, but entire colored bottles placed into the concrete itself; wonderful electric green and bright blue bottles adorned with more little chips of broken pieces of pottery. She has scratched into the concrete walls plant forms that she has later gone back and painted. Everything is lively, with these light catchers.

She has a pair of angels about fifteen feet tall that are on one of her chapels, blessing the space. Behind them are secret doors to more sacred spaces.

It's a terrible loss if people don't have the sense of the sacred. I have an idea that the place where

CULTIVATING
SACRED SPACE

God reveals himself most clearly now is in clouds. I watch them and make comments: "That was a little flat—I don't think it'll carry." I have several favorite patterns He creates with the clouds—it does make it kind of entertaining in another way besides the joy of just seeing beauty. It makes you aware this is not just an accident.

That's the greatest benefit of people taking art classes, if it opens their eye. It doesn't matter if they never paint or draw a thing. The joy of seeing—most people, it passes them by because they've never had to look closely.

🦋

Our gardens give us the opportunity to look intimately, to see the light and to lose ourselves in the creative process of making something beautiful.

▓

Rebecca Dye and Hank Helbush Gardens, Brookdale, California

Rebecca Dye and her husband, Hank Helbush, raise three children together and run a well-respected landscape architectural design firm. They both share a great love of one another, of family, of Nature, and of community. Their passionate love and enthusiasm is integrated with Nature into their personal lifestyle and their family values and how they run their business. We had a discussion about the natural gardens and environments they help create and how we can bring vitality back into our lives.

🦋

Hank: I think we ought to redefine what our quality of life is. It's not what we're told through the media to buy—it's being aware of what's around us.

Rebecca: The ideal place where many people want to live is where it's natural and wild and not all perfect and managed. They want to live in these naturally beautiful places, but when they go there, what do they do? They put in a lawn and a lot of little round hedges and shrubs. They want to be a part of it, but it's like they don't know how, so they keep nature at a distance, a "view," not a part of their life.

🦋

Hank and Rebecca's philosophy of creating their natural garden is more than a way to bring people back to the reality and beauty of the earth—for their own enrichment, it's also about helping the earth and all its creatures survive and thrive.

🦋

Hank: Sara Stine, who wrote a book called My Weeds, *realized after making an exquisite kitchen garden with parterres that she'd excluded all the animals—the animals had all left. Even the painted lady butterflies. She began to do a lot of research and she wrote her second book,* Noah's Garden, *that's like the cookbook of the world ecology. She had the insight to take information from all different disciplines and put them together. She looked at why birds migrate at a certain time of year and the connection of why some berries that the birds eat are ripe at the same time. There are all these different relationships she saw. What I've realized is that we must preserve the diversity of species in the environment we live in—our own gardens. It doesn't work to create these new villages—"developments"—with the ten best plants—best plants, meaning they have no pests, diseases, or animals—and then go to Yosemite for nature. We can't have this preserved open space and then these cities that are dead. We have to have a new vision about living within our environment. So what we need to do is preserve the species that are indigenous. I've done a lot of research on butterflies. They're very specific with host larval food. No matter how many butterfly bushes (Buddleia) you plant you're not going to get any "painted ladies" unless you have mallows for their larvae to eat. They aren't going to breed there, so they*

won't be preserved without plant and habitat diversity. By re-introducing or allowing the native plant species to come back, the animals are coming back, too, because then we're creating a sustainable environment. It's not sustainable if all the pieces aren't there.

🌿

Hank and Rebecca's philosophy is to embrace and enable Nature to bring her gifts back to the land. In their own personal garden, in a redwood forest that used to be an old camp for people to visit for the summer, a lot of invasive plants were planted, such as periwinkle vines and ivy as "groundcovers," which choked out delicate natives. So they removed the invasives and opened the soil up for Nature to come back in: for birds to plant the native seeds, for the seeds to find where they are best situated, to find where the water flows freely. Their creek floods and changes from one winter to the next, creating different little sandy banks where a rock or a log may have lodged, causing the water to change course. Rebecca explained some more of their philosophy:

🌿

The native grasses like fescue just started arriving. They shimmer in the light. So many birds have come since we took out the invasives. Native orange tigerlilies have been arriving—we've had to have patience, because the first year it was

CULTIVATING
SACRED SPACE

CULTIVATING
SACRED SPACE

Photograph by Rebecca Dye

pretty bare. Our hillside had an acre and a half of ivy growing on it. When we removed it, the wild seeds started germinating and it's like, who's going to show up? Who's coming?

🌿

They have helped their clients bring Nature back into their more mundane environments. So instead of just having a suburban kind of landscape of plain green lawn, they have called Nature back and given it the place. A rock farmer they work with goes up to a land full of huge boulders owned by a cattle rancher who wants some of them removed. The rock farmer carefully takes out some of the lichen covered rocks and brings them down to Rebecca and Hank's gardens. I asked Rebecca how she plants her stones—these great boulders they use in their landscaping projects.

🌿

Rebecca: First I have a general idea of the sizes and types of stone and the general locations where I want them in a particular garden. I make a list, like, one three-ton birdbath-shaped stone or an animal stone, or a four-ton one with low profile, and then the rocks just come. I figure whichever rocks want to come will come. I wait and see who comes. I don't pick them out. I send the list to the rock farmer, and the rocks come on huge flatbed trucks with moss and lichens and wildflowers. We handle them very

gently—not to scratch them—we sometimes have to go under electrical wires and through tree branches with big cranes. The scale and size are huge.

Certain rocks, when they arrive, you see families—sunny lichens, blue-green lichens, beautiful colors, ones with moss green colors and which ones probably came together, and you just know which ones want to be together, so then you think of them in relationships.

🌿

They place the rocks as though planting trees, in permanent places where the stones will live and grow. They want them to feel happy and natural there. They might put two rocks next to each other like kissing rocks and welcome the moss to grow on them.

🌿

Rebecca: You do it like flower arranging. I start with the biggest ones and any major ones that I know where I want to put them. Then all the others display themselves in relationship. I don't try to figure it out ahead anymore.

I'm always so delighted to see what arrives. We welcome them. Something that is really strange is that the rocks pull so much energy—and particularly on a sloping site when a new house has been put in and there's not enough room for the

Photograph by Rebecca Dye

energy to settle out. The energy runs down the hill. The rocks provide that power—to stabilize the energy that had dissipated off the site—even when they first arrive before they are set. The whole energy of the property changes. Everyone notices it. We all get incredibly thirsty. We have to drink lots of water all day. There seems to be a biological link with people, because even my monthly cycle will come whenever I set rocks. It's a natural biological connection, and we all feel how the energy changes

instantly. When the rocks are unloaded, everyone talks softly. It's like a Presence has arrived.

One of the most remarkable things Rebecca and Hank have created is an incredible stream. They placed rocks of all different sizes and shapes in a pattern, to be beautiful and natural, but also to create a variety of gurgling sounds, different kinds of drops of water, and changing movement. Then the stream was invited to run through the path created by the rocks.

Rebecca: It sounds like when you're up in the Sierra; there are shallow, wide washes with lots of little sounds and big spills and loud splashes. When you walk along it, all the sounds change. In the summertime when the banks are higher it's completely different than when the banks are more filled with water.

Hank: It's fun to move the boulders around and see how this changes the creek. It's the "hydro-ology" of the creek. Certain shapes make the *water dig down underneath; it changes the sound and the water patterns—it's all energy.*

All of a sudden, this landscape that would have been like a golf-course lawn was now alive, and crawfish, frogs, and fish came within days, sensing this was a place for them—a great blue heron flew in, and there is now singing and new life and babies. Inviting Nature back into these areas that were man-made, desolate places, renews the soul of the land as well as the soul of the people now on it. Hank and Rebecca's partnership is in life and in Nature. It began with wonder, and it is wonder that drives them now to create and share and believe.

Betty and Willis Peck's Gardens, Saratoga, California

Betty Peck, another dear friend, has worked all her life in bringing gardens to children. She founded and ran a community garden brimming with flowers, fruit, and vegetables. Six thousand children each year would come to learn, play, and work together as they celebrated every new sprout throughout the seasons for fifteen years. Betty says, "I consider every day precious, and count any day a child is not in the garden, one lost. And every day in the garden a celebration!"

Betty Peck, Ed.D., is a great lover and teacher of gardens. Her whole life has been about the garden. For more than fifty years she has brought gardening back to children in the kindergarten. Now she inspires, enriches, and instructs teachers in her own garden. Betty teaches the integration of all activities in the classrooms rooted and inspired by the garden: poetry, mathematics, singing games, reading, science, stories, cooking, social graces, art, music,

and meaningful artistic handwork. Even the teacher's dress and the decor of the classrooms are garden influenced, linked with the rhythm of the seasons, the phases of the moon, weekly garden chores, and daily discoveries and observations, helping the children develop and recognize their own personal rhythms.

Betty believes that the wisdom of the world is to be found in the garden: cultivating, planting, tending, and harvesting. She maintains that play is essential to the life of the child. The garden is not only the richest setting for play, it holds in secret all of life's lessons to be discovered by the child. The garden is the source of all art, and it is the stage for the child to develop not only his or her relationship to the earth but to the whole cosmos, coming into contact with the mystery of life.

I wish that every kindergarten door would open onto a garden to really learn what the world is all about. We were designed to be in the garden. Children need time for gathering wisdom— with no words, because words get in the way. Once the wisdom is gathered, the words will have meaning.

Through a garden gate with an arch covered with fragrant honeysuckle, we enter the children's vegetable garden. Betty believes that the need to "enter into" establishes a separation between what is and what could be. The child needs boundaries, as well as a beginning and ending. This establishes permission to begin anew. The opportunity for the sense of anticipation to form strong roots makes possible a lifetime of joy. Entering the garden gate brings with it a sense of anticipation as though entering a secret garden that holds unknown adventures.

The senses are all enriched in the garden: hearing bird calls, smelling fragrances, filling hungry eyes with beauty, feeling the textures and the joy of tasting.

Betty's vegetable garden has a birdbath and winding paths for processions. The paths are wheelbarrow-wide and are lined with fragrant plants like lavender and mints to feed the senses as you brush by to pick a wild strawberry. There are stumps about twelve inches high for children to sit on and look right into a flower's face. Betty says that the children look into the "Golden Center" of each flower and know that they're like the flowers because they have hearts of gold, too. This Golden Thread connects the children to feel their relatedness to Earth.

The stumps are small enough that the children can move them around themselves. When the stumps begin to decay they become mushroom and fungus farms, and all kinds of wonderful wigglies can be discovered underneath them.

Under a canopy of blooming trees there is a sandbox made from branches and natural sand, and shells to play with. Betty says:

🍃

Sand holds endless possibilities to develop the imagination. The building and rebuilding of everything that has been a part of their lives is a vital part of the sand play. Re-creating the world is the work of childhood. Sand belongs in the garden. It belongs in the garden for many reasons. One is that it forms the great waterways of the world. The rivers, lakes, streams, and oceans must be re-created, giving opportunity to understand the property of sand, water, rocks, and wood.

🍃

A beautiful throne made of bent willow canes is where Betty sits in the garden. She gathers the children around her for stories of the garden, peaceful activities, and songs. In Betty's kindergarten gardens and her home garden a rain barrel and a compost pile are as essential as teaching tools as the plants themselves.

🍃

To capture the rain is something a child can experience as caretakers of planet Earth. To be able to express gratitude to all who help capture the raindrops, sending this water to us to

CULTIVATING
SACRED SPACE

use, gives the child the opportunity to feel connected to the great forces of life. When they turn on the tap water, the children can then picture all that has gone into providing them with this water that is now theirs, and their "thank yous" fill the air.

❧

In Betty's kindergarten garden, one rain barrel of water a day was used any way the children liked. They learned to know that no raindrop is ever lost. The cycle of the raindrop's life becomes a vital part of their learning.

Compost is the gold of the garden. It is here that the child observes life into death and death into life. Therefore, it is centrally located in Betty's garden. Every leaf of the deciduous trees is claimed by the children. All cookie crumbs are put into the "Return to the Earth Bucket" inside the classroom or home. When it is full, it is carried out majestically by the children to place on the compost. Rabbit droppings, along with pony and horse manure, are added to the compost. "All things are all things" was an important message of the compost. During the spring the compost is

distributed to the garden in great ceremony. Pumpkin seeds are planted in the compost and left to grow over the summer months and harvested with delight in the autumn.

Betty also has a delightful little garden house, like a playhouse, and inside there are only books and stories about the garden and a big comfy chair with an appliquéd woman sitting on it called "Mother's Lap." If someone is feeling sad or lonely or needs to curl up in comfort, he or she can snuggle into the Mother's Lap, look into the garden through the vine-covered windows, pull out a gardening book, and read.

When Betty's little granddaughter Sarah started to learn to read, she would bring her books out into a tree where she would sit and read. Once Betty asked, "What would you like, Sarah?" and she replied, "Well, I wish this tree was a little bit more comfortable." So Betty built her a "Reading Treehouse" and put a little deck around the tree. The vines crawled over it for curtains, so now Sarah has her own secret place where she can enjoy her books amid Nature. It was in celebration of Sarah's new-found ability to read that Betty decided to name the different parts of her garden, each marked with a handmade sign.

Photograph by Hank Helbush

Betty has many elements in her garden. Her husband, Willis, and her son, Bill, are very much involved with theater, so they have built the "Theater of the Ground." It is a wonderful outdoor amphitheater with benches, a stage and antique white columns salvaged from an old southern mansion. Here friends gather to see lively performances. Willis is a lawyer, a historian, and a writer. He also loves trains, so he built his own train engine, put down tracks, and gives children and friends rides around the garden. He calls his small train station "Lower Expectation," which is worth considering because so often we have higher expectations and then greater disappointments. There is also a magnificent, big redwood tree called "The Call of the Wild," and that's where the children make their playhouses and little fantasy spots for the fairies and elves and for playing house. Above the river there is a spot with comfortable armchairs and a bench that's called "Cultural Change through Conversation." This is where friends gather to exchange ideas to help heal the world.

An open sunny spot is called "The Golden

Ring." It connects us to our golden hearts. This is where many ceremonies, teaching circles, and May Day dances take place. Annually, for over thirty years, this ancient rite has been celebrated by Betty and Willis, their children, friends, and students. Betty actually owns three maypoles: a portable one that she brings around with her, a hand-carved one that an artist friend made her that she used to bring to her community garden, and one that she grew herself in her schoolyard. One year I was honored to be the May Day Queen, to welcome the dancers and ask the piper and violinists to begin as the green and yellow ribbons were braided onto the maypole. Betty presided in her spring green dress. She served her traditional strawberry shortcake with cream, milked that morning from the last real home dairy in her area. Betty has introduced hundreds of children to the real work and magical wonders of this dairy. She and Willis, with their community, are now wholeheartedly saving this precious place from "development."

In my own childhood, the richest places in my life were the garden, the creek and hills, and a nearby dairy where we helped milk cows and feed chickens—and witnessed the birth and death of many animals. The smells, tastes, and exhausting play enriched my brothers and sisters and me for our entire lives. Now the dairyland we grew up with is part of the Golden Gate National Recreation Area, which has preserved thousands of acres for hiking and open space. I'm sure Betty and Willis's efforts to save their community dairy will succeed as their vision and celebrations for life have enriched so deeply all who know them.

Betty recently reminded me that the eternal human spirit gathers what is needed for its growth—like a flower unique in itself in what it gives and needs—and love and gratitude are what our souls need most. Being with Betty and Willis in their garden is an epiphany—a sudden, intuitive insight into the essential meaning of life through a simple yet deeply enriching experience.

✦

Lizzie's Garden of Memory, Monterey, California

I call my own personal garden "Lizzie's Garden of Memory" because it is full of plants I've loved since I was a child. When I first moved to this house seven years ago it had a garden of concrete, very invasive crabgrass, and trash. There was also one dying walnut tree whose limbs had been hacked into stumps. Bugs and woodpeckers riddled the gray bark with black holes. Eighteen huge black crows hung out in the branches cawing loudly at one another. My writing desk upstairs was at eye level with them—we would caw together. The crows would take green husked walnuts and drop them in the street when they saw cars coming. The cars would drive over them with a loud pop and crack, and the crows would crowd around the mashed nut and eat the meat!

California was in the middle of a long drought, so there were strict limitations on water usage. I had to plant carefully, using drought-resistant plants and drip irrigation. This was my first garden—for myself, in my own home—so I needed it to nurture me and to welcome children in.

My first priority was to work on the walnut tree: first to prune it properly—to give it respect. Many people would have removed it, but since it was the most prominent tree in the neighborhood (which was once an oak woodland), I prized it. On the side of the tree facing the sidewalk, there was a big, heart-shaped black hole where a limb had died. The neighborhood children and I recognized this as a fairy mailbox. The children made drawings, wrote notes, and placed offerings of flowers, shells, and favorite treasures in the hole. At night the flower fairies would come and get their mail and often leave tiny notes for

CULTIVATING
SACRED SPACE

the children. The notes were remarkable—tiny scraps of wrinkled-up paper, always written in tiny letters of green ink, then rolled up in miniature scrolls tied with golden thread. Each child took a flower name, which the fairies addressed them by.

This dialogue between the children and the fairies has inspired the children to make their own gardens so the fairies will come visit, and has inspired them to write and know about the other realms. It is the most wonderful aspect of the garden. Children I know in different regions are also discovering fairy mailboxes, and I'm told

there's quite a flurry of correspondence going on.

On Earth Day (April 22) about a month after I'd moved in, I hired Big John next door, who usually worked pouring cement, to bring a ninety-pound jackhammer to release the earth. It took two long days to break up the concrete. With the rubble I made a raised planter bed along the back of the property. Here I planted seven cypress trees to obscure the two-story-high apartment building that looked into the garden and my house.

The crabgrass was much harder to remove than the concrete; it has a nasty way of reappearing. Even the smallest piece, deep down, became a threat to take over—just like my old, unresolved issues that resurface and require more soil/soul work and weeding.

To invite the soul of the garden back in is a courageous act. Removing concrete that inhibits growth and warmth is very exciting. Possibilities require intention, care, and follow-through to activate. When we take off our own armor of protection we are more vulnerable, we can feel more deeply, and this can be painful—but then our own true, authentic self is revealed. The possibilities of growth are now endless. There may be messy, muddy times that are uncomfortable, or dormancy—when nothing seems to be happening and we need patience. The soul is now ready to receive. Growth has already begun below the surface as we open ourselves up to the light without the hard, impenetrable surface.

My garden is fenced in, and I wanted the walls to be living walls, not dead ones. I had holes cut in the concrete along the perimeters of the walls, and I planted apple trees and espaliered them along the east fence, providing a connection to the seasons, to change, and a time of fruition. Along the opposite wall I planted my favorite rose, Cécile Brunnér, the one with tiny, fragrant, pink roses. They have grown and covered the entire wall. As a small child I used to steal these roses from one of my neighbors to make little fairy crowns woven with blue forget-me-nots. The kind neighbor eventually dug up one of hers and gave this treasure to me. I was about six years old, and that was my first rosebush. The "little old ladies" in the neighborhood of my childhood invited me into their gardens and taught me the love of gardening. This in turn is what I do with my neighborhood children. I want a hospitable place for them, a place with enough abundance of flowers that they can pick flowers to bring home, pick them for the fairies, pick them for me, and still have plenty in the garden. I want lots of scents, wonderful fragrances to engage the children, so we planted chocolate peppermint to make tea and scented geraniums that smell like roses, lemons, and peppermint. These we call "magic leaves." When the children come in they know they may water with the old watering can and pick all the lavender they want. They also can draw pictures with chalk on the sidewalk and play some of the bamboo musical instruments around the garden.

The nasturtiums creep everywhere in my garden. I only planted a few seeds, but they have kind of taken over. They have such bright colors. The oranges and golds don't always blend with the other softer colors in the garden, but they are so cheerful. I can put them in salads and decorate my house with them, and they cover up the remaining cement walkways by creeping all over the place. In their modest way, they remind me of Monet's Grande Allée, so I love them very much.

Every year at the end of their cycle, when they get full of aphids, I pull them out and usually have about a five-gallon bucket of seeds that I can sweep up. I bring the seeds to the local school for classes to count, play with, and plant. The process becomes a whole lesson.

I have a working place in the garden, a little bench with little shrines around it. This is important because there is always potting and propagation to do. I like to have a place that is comfortable and pretty. The altar that came back with me from our wedding garden is in a promi-

nent sunny corner. It is important for me to have it with me. It's a place for offerings, rich with memories. The fire circle, the herbs, roses, and apple trees all have meaning, as do the musical instruments in the garden and places for the children to play. Bonsai pots that hold sand and pails of little toys are available for anyone to play with.

Over time, a garden takes on its own personality and expression. It's important to define its purpose and direction and invite nature to support our gardens. Because this is my sacred space of beauty and because I invite Nature to support my expression, I can't justify the use of chemicals, herbicides, or pesticides in it. I use my homemade compost to enrich the soil so it can promote and sustain healthy growth.

Now that I'm back in my own garden again—Gerald and I were together for two years before he died; then I came back to Monterey—I understand even better the relationship a person has to her garden. Some of the big trees and shrubs can survive without attention and love, but a lot of the special delicate plants that need tending can die out. But even if you don't tend your garden daily, you can admire it and think about it. You notice something beautiful in the garden every day. This feeling of appreciation and thankfulness gives energy to the plants and makes them happy. It's like having a conversation with them, a friendship.

When I returned to my garden, it had not been well cared for. A commercial "mow, blow, and go" gardener had come in and chopped the wonderful old rosemarys in half and pulled out all the lavenders and other precious wild things. He didn't know how to care for the old and wild. He

didn't have a kind, loving relationship with them. But I also realized that with love and an invitation to Nature spirits to return, the garden could again be imbued with spirit, beauty, and fun.

On the anniversary of Gerald's and my wedding, my friends and I had a celebration-of-life-and-love party. We had a fire circle where we put offerings of rosemary for remembrance into the flames and sat reading poems by the fire. We put up prayer flags across the back of the garden and set up one hundred glowing luminarias, made from white paper bags with sand inside, holding candles. The entire garden was lit with hundreds of tiny flames, some floating in the birdbath and others in paper lanterns hanging from trees and the luminarias in the paths. It was magical. The garden responded and is getting its spirit and beauty back again—and I am, too.

✦

Gerald Bol's Bamboo Sanctuary, Sebastopol, California

Gerald Bol, the Great Bamboo Man, fell in love with bamboo when he was a little boy and played with it in a neighbor's garden near his home in Palo Alto, California. When he moved to west Sebastopol thirty years ago he bought six acres very cheaply— a terrible piece of land that had been a gravel quarry. The land was completely ravaged and destroyed. The renters in the house had even chopped down oak and redwood trees—sacred, ancient trees—for firewood. They left garbage and had absolutely no respect for the land. When Gerald moved there, he started to take care of the soil. He first had to clean up the garbage and repair septic systems and get the well working. Over the years he redesigned the roads so they moved more gracefully on the land. He was trained as a painter and a sculptor, and in his heart he was also a botanist, scientist, and inventor. His art form became his garden. His sculpture was his land. With big bulldozers he resculpted this very sheer, very destroyed land, and with hard work and recycled materials (telephone poles and railroad ties) he terraced the land on a huge scale, built up the soil organically, and started to make gardens. Even after such incredible abuse, the soil was able to heal with the love and hard work of this devoted gardener.

After living on this land about fifteen years, Gerald rediscovered his great love of bamboo and grew five seeds, supposedly of a hardy timber bamboo, the giant kind that he had played with and made things out of as a child. When the plants developed he put one outside the greenhouse to see if it would take the frost, and it died. Then he knew it wasn't the seed he had thought and eventually identified it as a very rare and valu-

CULTIVATING
SACRED SPACE

able bamboo. He found a specialty plant nursery that was selling small specimens of this particular plant for $300 each, so he traded three of his plants and got a collection of twenty-five different bamboo species. There began his passion.

For the next fifteen years Gerald traveled around the world collecting bamboo, especially in Mexico and South America, where the native species grew in a dry Mediterranean climate similar to his own. He collected the bamboo from the wild, traveling by Jeep, donkey, and foot into remote areas with sketchy maps, hand-carrying it back. He had to comply with a USDA requirement that bamboo had to spend two years in quarantine before the plants were allowed into the country, to ensure they were free of nematodes or certain viruses that could harm agricultural crops such as wheat. Sometimes, of course, these rare plants died during quarantine, and this was a great disappointment.

Gerald was able to introduce some of the plants into the nursery trade for the first time. Bamboo is unusual in that some varieties only bloom every thirty or fifty years, and sometimes

you can't even decide what variety it is until it blooms. Then many varieties die once they've bloomed, and you have to regrow them by seed. So it takes great patience to work with bamboo, but patience is what Gerald had. Ultimately he collected and cultivated 350 varieties in his garden. He began to grow bamboo up and down the sheer hillsides, on the terraced gravel beds. He planted the bamboo with ornamental grasses with different colors, from acid yellow to soft pink and black. This resulted in wonderful textures and patterns in his demonstration gardens.

The arching bamboo created swaying tunnels, which lead one to raised islands of bamboo covered with baby tears. He cut away little channels in the ground for springs and waterways to move through and covered them with flat stones for small bridges. It was a practical solution for muddy soil, but also very beautiful, with the feeling of a traditional Japanese garden.

Throughout the year the garden has great interest because the bamboo, of course, keeps its form, but the wide variety of ornamental grasses change both form and color. Gerald made bamboo

fences and gateways and placed benches in secret little places next to the stream and on cliffs. Here one could sit in a protected, secret area surrounded with foliage and look at the view in the distance of big forests of timber bamboo. His bamboo grew everywhere, alongside towering redwood trees, scented bay trees, lichen-covered oak trees, and fruit trees laden with pears, persimmons, and plums. The bamboo rhizomes grow only about six to eight inches deep, so Gerald discovered he could grow timber bamboo thirty feet tall on top of gravel in beds of good soil, the depth of just a railroad tie. Then he could cut it out like a piece of pie to transplant or sell easily.

Gerald's personal passion for bamboo became an international treasure. He started his nursery, "Bamboo Sourcery," so that he could afford to keep up his immense garden and also share his great love of bamboo with others. People from Japan, Europe, and all over the United States came to his bamboo gardens to learn about bamboo, to buy it, and to see it in these most unusual settings. It was magical. Rare endangered birds came to Gerald's transformed gravel quarry and found sanctuary there. Huge pileated woodpeckers made their homes in the tall fir trees, bluebirds nested among the apple trees, and many small, colorful migratory birds found refuge among the bamboo. They added their songs to the rustle of the bamboo leaves and the free-flowing stream, no longer blocked by

debris, where the Native Americans had once carved bowls in the bedrock to leach their acorns. Fresh water always rose from this deep source—even during times of drought.

So the land breathed something special, and Gerald brought his bamboo—the plant that connects Heaven and Earth—and his vision together, and something very special grew.

<hr />

Lily Yeh: The Village of Arts and Humanities, Philadelphia, Pennsylvania

When the spirit of the land has been destroyed or buried in cities, and where destruction and disrespect is common, gardens from the heart can restore the gardener, the land, and the surrounding areas. Passionate artists and gardeners find a way to instill beauty and individuality, while respecting Nature.

Transformation can occur in any environment. We can look to the example of those who garden in inner-city empty lots, beautifying and unifying neighborhoods. Creative gardeners can envision the transformation of space and how to grow trees, flowers, herbs, even water gardens, in order to restore a connection with Nature and cultivate a personalized view of Paradise.

Lily Yeh is a modern-day alchemist. She has

transformed the rubble of north Philadelphia's "Badlands" into soul, spirit, and beauty. Empty lots piled with trash and debris were physical metaphors for the empty souls in this ghetto neighborhood. As a Chinese landscape-painter-turned-installation-artist looking for more meaningful work, Lily Yeh was offered an empty lot in north Philadelphia to use for her artistic statement in 1985.

❧

I didn't know how to do it. . . . I was scared, being an Asian woman—I'd be an outsider, and people said, "Don't come, they'll destroy the work," and I almost bowed out. But I felt there was a voice in me and if I didn't rise to the occasion, the best part of me would die.

In the beginning I had no idea what to do. I bought rakes and shovels and began with a circle in the center. Children came to help; the energy and feeling was great. I felt I'd planted a seed. So, I've come back. We call it a village

because the center, our focus, is right here.

We transform the neighborhood and through that we build people and we heal from the bottom up.

❧

The Village of Arts and Humanities began with one empty lot and now, over the last ten years, fifty-five abandoned properties have been successfully transformed into parks, gardens, education facilities, offices, and low-income housing. This has made the Village an oasis of trees, flowers, murals, and brightly colored mosaics and has enriched the lives of hundreds of children, unemployed adults, and anyone else the project touches.

Lily was quite aware of the dangers of the neighborhood and decided that the Village needed some protection. Between two buildings she painted angels bigger than life. Her designs were not from the lightweight, all-white Victorian cherubs we are all inundated with, but with strong, powerful, warrior-type angels inspired by Ethiopian icons, images that were strong enough to protect and that the neighborhood could relate to. She introduced the art of mosaic to the unemployed neighbors who had plenty of time on their hands. James "Big Man" Maxton, a recovering substance abuser, learned to take the shattered pieces of tile and set them in the beautiful angel patterns, imbuing them with greater beauty, meaning, and longevity, and at the same time bringing the scattered pieces of his own life into a gathered whole. He now is a skilled mosaic artist and teaches others. He says,

The Village for me has been an oasis of culture, and full of colors in an area of desolation and decay. It is a maze of wonder in this dilapidated inner city area. And for that I am truly blessed.

I heard Lily Yeh speaking at an inspirational conference called "Transcending Contemporary Taboos: Reawakening to Beauty, Wonder, and Sacred Values Through the Arts," presented at the Cathedral of St. John the Divine in New York City by the organization Sacred in the Arts. I felt thoroughly inspired by Lily's all-encompassing transformation and went to visit the Village.

When I walked in "Angel Alley," I was overwhelmed with the beauty and strength of the angels. I was struck by their black and red faces, colorful clothes, and swords mosaicked with bits of mirror. The shining sword blades can reflect back any negativity that is directed their way. The swords are also for cutting through the nonessential.

At first there was no budget for trees in the Village, so the participants decided to create them. Lily got concrete to make into tree forms and painted them—but the paint chipped off, so they learned to mosaic them. They then transformed some into their own personal totems (see page 52). It wouldn't have made sense for the people of this area to have carved wooden totems like those of the Pacific Northwest (there are no big trees available for such a purpose), so they created their own of mosaic and concrete. Big Man made a totem in honor of his mother, who had recently died. Lily says,

So from nothing we can make wonderful things, and that's what we want to teach our children. Our Village motto is "Kujenga Pamoja." It is Swahili and means "Together we build."

One of the most beautiful spots in the Village is the meditation park. An old derelict building covered over with plaster displays a

CULTIVATING
SACRED SPACE

huge, striking Tree of Life mosaic in the middle, a star-lit blooming tree, in a courtyard all mosaicked with circular patterns of blues and greens or reds and oranges—the warm and the cool right next to one another. I had never seen the Tree of Life portrayed in such a gorgeous setting, and I have never seen one that gives more vitality to the place and the people than the one in the Village of Arts and Humanities.

The focus of the village is not just about making mosaics. It is about taking the disjointed, broken pieces of people's lives and making them into a creative, beautiful, and meaningful whole, forging a community of compassion, renewal, and celebration.

The children participants of the Village gather life stories of the elders and transform them into plays and dances to perform for the neighborhood. Art projects for children have included painting more angels on the walls for protection in their own special garden. The children pressed themselves against the walls

and someone outlined them, making their hands into great wings.

❦

The Village means everything to me.
—Maurice Phillips, age 8

❦

The teens successfully completed the first year of The Rites of Passage Program, which included writing, photography, theater arts, job training, and crafts. The program culminated with the play "A Different Place in Time," performed and partially created by the youth in the program. The Village has since increased its Education through Art program for children. Enrollment rose to over one hundred in its core program in 1996. An additional four hundred children participate in the Village's outreach program.

The Magical Garden in the Village has a sixty-by-twenty-foot mural and a community flower garden. The mural contains large, fanciful, geometrically shaped flowers with stylized human, animal, and insect figures. Lily's sources of inspiration have been wall paintings from African and Indian villages and tiled murals from the Middle East. She is also incorporating images and motifs created by children at the Village's various workshops. They have launched a craft project in which these images are transformed into

highly marketable items by professional artists and designers. The production includes greeting cards, hand puppets, dolls, figurines, mobiles, and booklets.

What better way could there be to make a healing garden than through awakening the souls of the children? Through their effervescent spirits life truly renews. The laughter of children has brought vitality back. Like sunshine, the sweet warmth shimmers and sparkles and opens the way. A painted mural of a phoenix rising up from the ashes appears on a three-story building, a living symbol of the Village.

The neighborhood resident workers are impressed by the beauty of the village and energized by its vision. They share an intense sense of pride, knowing that they have created a place of beauty and magic. They even built a sculptured, handmade oven to bake community bread to feed the Village's body and soul.

The people here have a sense of joy and purpose back in their lives. Through grants and donations, residents of the neighborhood also make up the paid crews that have restored the falling-down buildings. Now there are more art workshops, a teen center for pottery and painting, and a light-filled gallery to display neighborhood art. There are dance classes, theatrical productions, and lessons as varied as "how to use a computer" to "how to cook." Artists and volunteers from all

over put in hundreds of hours in the Village, thrilled to be a part of this transformative power through art.

The Village is the best of the best. . . . I cannot speak about it without tears welling up.
—*Ali Wagner, Philadelphia fabric artist*

This is now a fertile sacred ground, seeding and feeding the entire Village. The soils and souls are being replenished. Impoverished places and people are sustaining growth, beauty, and renewal. The life-death struggle has been transformed back to new life.

AUTUMN

Autumn is such a full, rich season. Its beauty comes from its ripeness and maturity. It is a time of harvest, feasting, celebration, and gratitude for all the abundance. Yet in the midst of bushels of apples and piles of raked-up, crunchy leaves there is the deep realization that at the height of fruition we are also nearing winter. Autumn is the season of letting go, as once again there will be dormancy. This is the time to put food by—drying, canning, freezing—and prepare for the long, cold nights ahead.

❀

AUTUMN FLOWERS ARE OFFERED IN A RAKU POT AT THE
ENTRANCE TO THE WEDDING GARDEN.

Photograph by Lyn Sweeney

When we create our sacred space we may include some of the ideas, inspirations, ancient wisdom, and archetypes gathered in other seasons. But to bless the space and invoke it with meaning and memory, we must also create our own celebrations, ceremonies, and rituals. These occasions can be centered around the seasons or around the great events in our lives, such as birth, marriage, and death. They can include elements from different cultures and spiritual traditions, or we can make them up out of our imagination—whatever resonates in us and rings true. When our hearts feel touched we know that our ceremonies are authentic. The dual characteristics of autumn—bounty of the harvest and preparation for dormancy—make it a rich season for creating ritual.

✿

Gerald and I designed and made our wedding garden in the spirit of our love, a truly personal sacred space where we could welcome friends and family to join us in our blessed union and celebration. We began with a dream Gerald had after his former wife died that gave him great comfort. In this dream he saw a pebble dropping into a still pool, and radiating from the plopping pebble were rings of radiance symbolizing the continuum of love.

The process of making our own sacred garden within Gerald's bamboo sanctuary, the land

that he had lived and worked on for thirty years, was a collaboration and a vision that combined both of our creative spirits. It was part of the process of joining our lives and souls. We had envisioned that in the future it could be a place for teaching and other healing practices, as well as a place for communion with friends and family. Both of our lives had been so deeply touched by loved ones dying that we thought this would be something we could do together to help people on the threshold of death, and those in the healing grief process after death. We wanted the garden to be an example of our love and a place with a higher purpose.

We began our garden with a distinctive white stone circle. At the heart of the circle Gerald laid a fire pit with stones layered as in a kiva. A wooden deck covered the pit. We constructed a raised stone terrace—to compensate for the sloping site—around the pit. A curved path led to a roofed, bamboo gate, beyond which were thirty benches built by Gerald and his foreman. The bench supports came from a huge Douglas fir that had fallen the previous winter, and the tops of the benches were made from the crossbars of recycled telephone poles, all sanded. The design was like an inverted amphitheater—with the raised terrace like a stage. We chose weathered stones to work with that already had lichen on them. We built a dry stone wall to support the base of the terrace,

Wedding altar, photograph by Lyn Sweeney

steps, and path, and planted creeping thyme, sedums, and many small herbs and alpine plants between the cracks of the terrace.

Before we left on our "pre-honeymoon" trip to Bali and Japan, a friend suggested we engage a caterer for our wedding. Gerald said, "Use a caterer?! Wouldn't the biggest gift of love we could give our friends be to cook delicious food for them?" More than twenty years before when Gerald was my college art teacher, he had invited me with other students to this same land, terraced with his organic vegetable gardens, to help make an Indonesian *Rijstafel,* a feast of twenty intricate dishes. So typically, rather than simplifying, Gerald and I expanded and conjoined our creative ideas and energies. We became inspired to make this feast again and invite our friends to come days ahead to help prepare our wedding banquet and imbue our sacred space with their love and energy. We left for Bali, to attend the International Bamboo Congress, and then for Japan, to share together places and people we knew and loved.

T. WILSON 97

CULTIVATING
SACRED SPACE

We knew we wanted to include sacred elements in our wedding celebration, such as bamboo structures, plants, and utensils and a water basin for purifying at the garden entrance. So as we traveled we collected rare Indonesian spices, batiks for clothing and for covering the feast tables, Bali flags in a range of rainbow colors, and three sacred umbrellas in gold and white for our procession and decoration. We also sent back many handmade Balinese bamboo musical instruments such as flutes and gamelans. We envisioned a joyous ceremony of love and celebration in which everyone could participate.

After we returned home, the elements of the ceremony itself began to emerge through our combined vision. The fire pit would be a central feature, symbolic of keeping the marriage kindled, an eternal flame of creative passion and love. I felt strongly about making an altar. We found a wonderful piece of stone, and Gerald cut more logs from the fallen tree for the legs. On this altar we would put the offerings for the wedding, pomegranates and kiwis and fruits and flowers that we had grown in our own garden.

We planted a meadow mix of wildflower seeds and grasses to soften the edges of the garden and mulched the paths with recycled wood chips. With all the bamboo we wanted, it was easy to bring containers from the nursery stock to screen the house and work areas. Open lattice bamboo fences were made to enclose the space.

We completed all of this weeks ahead. Planning our ceremony, writing our vows, making our rings from bamboo rhizomes cast into gold, making and sending out our invitations, and coordinating the preparation of the feast also needed much time and consideration.

Gerald was in charge of the food with many friends assisting him. The main course would be venison, heart meat of the Native American Indians, and salmon, the sacred fish of knowledge for the Celts (caught and barbecued by my brother Matt). It was an enormous project full of loving detail and beauty.

Many dear friends and family arrived days early from all over the world, including Mark Brown from France and Thomas Gröner and Ziglinda from Germany, who helped make the magnificent flower decorations and offerings. They created for me a twelve-foot-long bouquet designed to trail behind me like a flower train in the wedding procession. It was woven with golden threads, lace, ribbons, jewels, roses, wild passion vines, berries, and light-reflecting lunaria—like small, full moons. Gerald would wear a graceful, long garland fashioned from his climbing bamboo that he had brought back from Chile, wound and woven with roses and silk ribbons.

We gathered bamboo poles to be used for gates, flagpoles, umbrella handles, and arches over our wedding site. Bud vases were made by cutting sections of bamboo between the nodes;

Bamboo bud vases, photograph by Lyn Sweeney

small holes were drilled at the top so they could be tied onto posts and poles, gates and thresholds. Though they were only small details, they were a delight to the eye. Layers of details add great richness and depth and are best when not too fussy and blended so well that they are hardly noticed. Thoughtful details don't call attention to themselves; they just quietly breathe more life—like all the layered details on the mossy floor of a forest.

Everyone who wanted to was able to create or contribute something. Tibetan prayer flags and silk rainbow ribbons were hung across the canyon below the garden. Bamboo culms were added to the main entrance gate for a sculptural free-form feeling, friends made music, and flower lovers were able to weave wreaths for the children's hair or help with decorations on the table settings and all around the grounds. With this activity we all got to know each other more, and we all had a

Photograph by Anna Rheim

deeper appreciation and a sense of cooperation in creating the sacred together. It brought our diverse lives and varied friends and family together in a wonderful, celebratory way. And Gerald and I, both as teachers and artists who love to make the space for creativity, were both so delighted and happy with how this emerged. There wasn't a sense of competition or strong ordering around of things. Preparing for the wedding was a real collaboration and so much more gratifying than it would have been if we had hired caterers and organizers. It created more love, and the layers of beauty and generous thoughtfulness imbued and enriched all of us. This was more than we could ever have done ourselves or anticipated.

In the ceremony we wanted to be able to include everyone, and especially we wanted to honor the young children in our lives: my niece, Rebecca; Gerald's two granddaughters, and other little friends of mine that had been a part of my fairy gardens and who were very close to me. So we invited them to be flower fairies in our wedding. Sasha, Gerald's daughter-in-law, made them beautiful little costumes, and I constructed magic wands out of sunflowers with little dangly flowers attached with silver wires. There were seven flower fairies and two angels. They had the very special job of entering the garden and, with their flower wands, bringing in their magic and their love, sanctifying the sacred space for our marriage. So they

led the procession inward, and all those in the procession washed their hands at the garden entrance gate. A bamboo flutist played Balinese music throughout. On the way to the garden, Gerald and I stopped at the shrine of his late wife and gave our offerings.

Gerald's son and two stepchildren held the sacred umbrellas from Bali in the procession, and various friends and family members held the eighteen different colored flags, and then placed them around the garden to bring up the ch'i and to add beautiful color and movement, helping to hold the space together. The golden umbrellas stood over the two of us and the white one over the priest who married us.

❦

As it turned out, with Gerald's very sudden and severe illness, it was a great gift that we had had such an amazing wedding, because it united our deep love and the tender nurture and overwhelming resource of love from others that Gerald and I had already gathered. It had touched both of us, our friends, and our families. Two and a half months after our wedding, we found out that Gerald had a brain tumor and had to have a horrible operation immediately. After surgery, we spent weeks in the hospital, and he had to completely learn to talk and walk and eat again. It was the love of our friends and family that helped sustain us and give us the strength to go through these fires.

The garden was a place of love and tranquility for Gerald. He looked at it in photographs when he was in the hospital, and later from his oval window in the house. When he got better he'd use the walker or his canes and we'd go down into the garden—a big accomplishment—and weed together in our sacred circle. Weeding our circle gave him a sense of purpose and contribution. He also got energy from this place that we had created for our love and with our love. In this way the garden was healing.

One day when Rebecca, who was five years old, came to visit us, she and I went to the garden and I explained to her that Gerald had been going there to weed as part of his healing. There was a big camellia shrub nearby, full of pink and white blossoms. She said, "Lizzie, give me just the pink ones," and I gave her a whole apron full of them. She created a circle of pink blossoms on top of the white stone circle. Then she said, "Lizzie, this is a healing circle, and when Gerald comes down here, if he goes into the circle he can get healed." We put blossoms on the altar as an offering, and she did a little dance, throwing up the pink and white petals in the center—like a prayer dance. She had just made that up and it was so sweet and pure; her spontaneity and love were part of the healing. Sadly it wasn't a physical healing, but it was a healing of spirit and of soul.

Other times, when Gerald was up to it, I'd

bring him in the car to visit the bamboo he so loved. We would sit among it and watch it grow—some shoots can grow six inches a day! When the bamboo culms were being rooted and growing in the greenhouse, we'd be surrounded with vital growth energy. (For the big timber bamboo, it is the *old* rhizomes, the old roots, that shoot out the huge culms, sometimes five or six inches in diameter. The new rhizomes only produce skinny little pieces of bamboo. Unlike trees, the girth of bamboo doesn't develop in rings of growth—the increase in size of the culm comes from the maturity of the rhizome. It's out of maturity that the greatness comes. This is a wonderful metaphor for us, because when we age and get more wisdom, our full potential can be realized.)

It was extremely difficult to witness the physical decline of Gerald during his illness because he was such a vital, strong person, and we had so much looked forward to being together for a long time. During his radiation treatments he lost his thick, black hair, and he lost over fifty pounds because he couldn't eat. His spine was marked with blue points for the treatments to be precise; I thought with shock that he looked like he had suffered the tortures of Auschwitz. Then I realized he was a victim of a war, and it was the war on cancer. With his diminishing body, his spirit continued to grow strong and loving, and his radiance of love predominated. I had seen this before when

Photograph by Anna Rheim

Rebecca's mom, Pam, my dear sister-in-law, died. The body fades and becomes transparent, and the spirit shines forward. You can clearly see the separation—soul from body. And so I believe that the soul continues to exist after death.

When Gerald died, it was actually a great shock and completely unexpected. We had been told that he was going to live, that he had an 80 percent chance of survival, and all the medical people kept saying he was going to get better. Sometimes I would notice that his spirit would drift away, and I would feel like he might be preparing to die; and yet the doctor said, five days before he died, "Oh no, he's going to get better." Gerald and I made happy, healing plans.

When he died very quickly and unexpectedly from a brain embolism, I was with him to love, fight for him, and then let him go. He died in the emergency room, and I insisted on bringing his body home to have a wake. This apparently was an unusual request, and I had to go through the county coroner for permission. I was adamant. We arranged transportation with the Neptune Society to bring him home, and I put him in our bed. My friend Yvonne and I had painted a life-size angel above the bed as a guardian healing angel, inspired by Lily Yeh's angels for protection. I had helped wash Gerald at the hospital and now I anointed him with lavender oil, an old custom for helping preserve the body—the scent is soothing and relaxing.

Our friends and family came to say good-bye to him, and I made a large bamboo garland, like the one he wore at our wedding, with roses friends brought from their gardens woven in. When Rebecca came, she sat on the bed with me next to Gerald and said, "Oh Lizzie, he's so beautiful. He looks so beautiful, Lizzie, and today is such a special day. It's so special because we are all so sad. And we are all so sad because it is our last day with Gerald." And it was our last day with him in his physical form, but, like leaving the garden, his energy and love has continued to nurture and enrich me. I have endless golden treasures I will always value stored in my "temple of memory."

For the wake we kept the fire burning in our wedding garden. It was the first time that a fire had been lit there. I hadn't realized it, but in Mexico that is the tradition, that when someone you love dies you make a fire and you sit with the fire and you let it burn all night. You keep feeding it, you gather around it, and you talk about the person who died. It's a way to comfort one another as you light a path for the soul that has been called away. So that's what was done, and Gerald's nursery foreman and crew kept the fire burning all night, and I kept Gerald company all night. In the morning he was smiling. It was very unusual. And his heart chakra had kept warm, even though the rest of his body had gotten cold.

I wanted to have his memorial in our garden.

Photograph by Anna Rheim

Sadly, it was only eight months after our wedding. But our garden was the appropriate place because it was here we had gathered our friends in love. The garden had been part of Gerald's healing, and it was the central point of our creative life together.

We gathered baskets and filled them with offerings: one with rosemary, because it is about remembrance and remembering; one with bamboo, the connection of heaven and earth; another with pieces of sage, for purification; and one with pieces of cedar, for clarity. Friends were invited to throw these offerings into the fire. We also had small squares of joss paper, adorned with gold leaf, from China; we wrote down our wishes and prayers on them and threw them on the fire, too.

People sang songs and told stories about Gerald. The bamboo flutist who had played at our wedding came again to play—the sweet soul music of Bali from an instrument made from the plant Gerald loved the most. Afterward we had a feast with all the foods that he liked the best. Some of his old kinetic sculptures that he had made in the '60s were resurrected: the heat from

CULTIVATING
SACRED SPACE

Photograph by Rebecca Dye

a fire lit inside of them made them move and make funny sounds, a testament to Gerald's genius and humor. Gerald also loved making his own fireworks, so his friends got together and re-created these fireworks, setting them off at dusk to send his spirit soaring into the starlit heavens. It was truly a celebration of Gerald's life.

A garden is a place where we are invited to make a relationship with nature. A sacred space in a garden needs to be made with great love and with great intention and commitment. I think it is most powerful and meaningful when we invite in friends and family members that we love, and with their energy the sacredness of the garden comes to life even more. There is a love that can be kindled between two people that is regenerative; it is healing; it is like the love that we can feel from the divine or the great spirits, the Creator, the regenerative powers that are in the universe. Two people can create that love between themselves, and it can radiate outward—like the circles created by the pebble in the pond—and affect many people as it deepens within our own selves. This kind of love is healing. Even if the body cannot be healed from a major disease, the spirit can be healed. Old wounds can be healed, and the soul can be healed, and love continues to nurture even when we don't see the source.

When we truly feel a comfort and a relation-ship in Nature, this gives us regeneration. This gives us the link to the life-death-life cycle. And gardens provide us the opportunity to have a deep relationship with Nature. In this way, with our love we can know the eternal. We can actually be a part of the continuum of the universe. We can make beautiful places where we feel the healing in ourselves and others—where joy is sparked and where renewal happens. Like any spiritual work, it can't just be done once and then left. It is a daily process.

I get very sad when people in the vitality of their lives die. Yet when the fruit is early and ripe on the trees or on the vine, and the harvest is sweet and early, this is a time for celebration; it is not a time for mourning. When the soul of some-one is fully realized and is ready to leave this life experience, it is also an early harvest.

Sometimes when you see a very wilted flower that has fallen out of a vase of water, you can take that flower and instead of just throwing it away, you can re-cut the stem and place it in fresh water, and it will get rejuvenated. It will become beautiful and full and open again. This is what happens to our souls with love and with beauty. And this is what can happen in the gar-den, when we're close to Nature and we're surrounded by this beauty. When our souls feel weary and wilted, they can become regenerated. It is also what happens to the soil itself; when it has been trashed and cemented over—like in Lily

Yeh's inner city plot in Philadelphia, or like Gerald's reclaimed land, which had been raped and abused for a gravel pit—and then new life emerges; the moisture comes back. With sunshine and love and radiance, new life happens and new blossoms come forward: there is a renewal. With that renewal we can also be nurtured by our experiences, by our past. Like compost, our experiences can be part of the source, the dark depth that our roots draw from. This is where compassion and empathy come from. It is the source of our growth and it teaches us how to nurture ourselves.

I have learned about infinity, the life-death-life cycle, from Nature. When something dies, whether it is a tree on the forest floor or a cutting from my garden thrown in the compost pile, it breaks down. It changes form and creates richness and food for the rest of life—insects, little worms and bugs. Trees get nurture from this breaking down, mushrooms come—animal life feeds off all of that. The same is true with our love. It keeps regenerating. When someone dies, they're not really gone completely. Their energy continues, and it continues to nurture us. We can draw from that. In this way we can come to know the eternal, the continuum of life.

CULTIVATING
SACRED SPACE

The Wild Has No Formula

Spontaneously
surviving

Beauty
Nurtures
Nature

Nature
Nurtures
Soul

Sun warms
    Earth
     Supports

Green
    sprouts
    Feed soil
    Soul feeds
Expression

    Rain
    Falls

Water
Fills
    Full-Fills

Well
    Wellness

Deep
    Dark
        Depth
          Feeds soul-soil

CULTIVATING
SACRED SPACE

Gardens to Visit

Saihoji Temple (Kokedera Temple)

56 Kamigaya-cho, Matsuo, Nishigyo-ku, Kyoto 615, Japan The temple is a fifteen-minute walk from Kami-Katsura Station on the Hankyu Arashiyama Line. Admission: 3,000 yen. Advance booking by mail is necessary (enclose an addressed and stamped return postcard).

Bali

For a special Bali experience, visiting gardens and artists' homes and staying with dancers, painters, and healers, contact Cok Ratih SE, Ji. Raya Legran No. 118, Kuta, Bali, Indonesia; telephone (62 361) 262451, FAX (62 361) 754201.

Abby Aldrich Rockefeller Garden

Open Thursdays in July by appointment only. Write to the garden at Seal Harbor, P.O. Box 206, Mt. Desert Island, Maine; or call in May for an appointment, (207) 276-3330.

In nearby Maine:

Thuya Garden is part of a park known as Asticou Terraces in Northeast Harbor on Mt. Desert Island, Maine. It is well worth a visit.

Musée Claude Monet

27620 Giverny, France Open Tuesday through Sunday, 10 a.m. to 6 p.m., April 1–October 31 Take a train from Paris at Gare St. Lazare to Vernon, direction Rouen. From Vernon take a taxi, bicycle, or walk two and a half miles to Giverny.

While in Giverny, also see:

Musée Américain Open April through October This museum houses an outstanding collection of American Impressionist paintings done in Giverny during the time Monet lived there.

Musée Hôtel Baudy Open summer months Renoir, Sisley, Pissarro, and Cézanne stayed here and painted while visiting Monet. The charming garden around the old painters' studio is full of old-fashioned roses.

Lilla Cabot-Perry Garden Lilla Cabot-Perry was an American Impressionist who lived next door to Monet. Mark Brown restored her magnificent garden.

Esalen Institute

Highway 1, Big Sur, CA 93920-9616

For general information and reservations, call (408) 667-3000. Catalogs on residential workshops are available.

Mark Brown's Garden

Open by appointment only.

Write to La Berquerie, 76119 Varengeville-sur-Mer, France.

Also in Varengeville-sur-Mer, near Dieppe on the Normandy Coast:

Le Bois des Moutiers

76119 Varengeville-sur-Mer;

telephone 35-85-10-02

Open March to November, these magnificent gardens that extend to the sea were influenced by garden designer Gertrude Jekyll. The stunning house at the site was built by Sir Edwin Lutyens.

Near Varengeville:

Le Vasterival

76119 Sainte-Marguerite-sur-Mer;

telephone: 35-85-12-05

Visits by appointment only. These spectacular gardens made by Princesse Sturdza cover twenty acres by the sea with collections of rhododendrons, hydrangeas, and acers, among other botanical specimens radiant with beauty.

Rebecca Dye and Hank Helbush, Landscape Architects

Design Focus, P. O. Box 605, Saratoga, CA 95071; telephone: (408) 867-3747, FAX (408) 867-3774

Betty Peck, Ed.D.

14275 Saratoga Avenue, Saratoga, CA 95070

Betty is also a consultant for designing children's play gardens as well as gardens and classrooms for kindergartens.

Bamboo Sourcery

666 Wagnon Road, Sebastopol, CA 95472; telephone (707) 823-5866

Visit by appointment only.

Mail-order catalog: $3.00.

For more information about bamboo: American Bamboo Society, 750 Krumkill Rd., Albany, NY 12203-5976; telephone (518) 458-7618, FAX (518) 458-7625

The Village of Arts and Humanities

Lily Yeh, Executive Director

2544 Germantown Avenue, Philadelphia, PA 19133; telephone: (215) 225-7830, FAX (215) 225-4339

Tax-deductible contributions are welcome to continue their programs and projects. Visitors are welcome by appointment.

Recommended Reading and Resources

Anderson, Kat. *Before the Wilderness: Environmental Management of California Natives.* Menlo Park, Calif.: Ballena Press, 1993.

Arrien, Angeles. *The Four-fold Way: Walking the Path of the Warrior, Teacher, Healer and Visionary.* San Francisco: Harper, 1993.

Artress, Dr. Lauren. *Walking a Sacred Path: Rediscovering the Labyrinth as a Spiritual Tool.* East Rutherford, N.J.: Putnam, 1995.

Barker, Cicely Mary. *Flower Fairies of the Spring.* London: Blackie & Son Ltd., n.d.

Bird, Christopher, and Peter Tompkins. *Secrets of the Soil.* New York: Harper & Row, 1989.

Brusatin, Manlio. *A History of Colors.* Boston: Shambhala, 1991.

Chaplin, Mary. *Gardening for the Physically Handicapped and Elderly.* London: Batsford Ltd., 1980.

Ching, Ni Hua. *The Book of Changes and the Unchanging Truth.* Los Angeles: Shrine of the Eternal Breath of Tao, 1990.

Fasset, Kaffe. *Glorious Inspiration: Sources from Art and Nature for Innovative Needlework Design.* New York: Clarkson Potter, 1991.

Franck, Frederick. *The Zen of Seeing.* New York: Random House, 1973.

Henri, Robert. *The Art Spirit.* New York: Harper Collins, 1984.

Hobhouse, Penelope. *Color in Your Garden.* Boston: Little, Brown & Co., 1985.

Hobhouse, Penelope, ed. *Gertrude Jekyll on Gardening.* New York: Vintage Books, 1985.

Hoff, Benjamin, ed. *The Singing Creek Where the Willows Grow: The Rediscovered Diary of Opal Whiteley.* New York: Ticknor & Fields, 1986.

Itten, Johannes. *The Art of Color.* New York: Van Nostrand Reinhold, 1973.

Jarman, Derek. *Derek Jarman's Garden.* New York: Overlook Press, 1995.

Jekyll, Gertrude. *Color Schemes for the Flower Garden.* Salem, N.H.: Ayer Co., 1983.

————. *The Making of a Garden.* Woodbridge, England: Baron Publishing, 1984.

————. *Wall & Water Gardens.* Salem, N.H.: Ayer Co., 1983.

————. *Wood and Garden.* Salem, N.H.: Ayer Co., 1983.

Jekyll, Gertrude, and Edward Mawley. *Roses.* Salem, N.H.: Ayer Co., 1983.

Jekyll, Gertrude, and Lawrence Weaver. *Gardens for Small Country Houses.* Woodbridge, England: Baron Publishing, 1981.

Kleinman, Kathryn, and Michaele Thunen. *Souvenirs: Gifts from the Garden.* San Francisco: Collins, 1994.

Landau, Dianna, and Shelby Stump. *Living with Wild Life: How to enjoy, cope with, and protect North America's wild creatures around your home and theirs.* San Francisco: Sierra Club Books, 1994.

Levine, Stephen and Ondrea. *Embracing the Beloved: Relationship as a Path of Awakening.* New York: Doubleday, 1995.

London, Peter. *No More Secondhand Art.* Boston: Shambhala Publications, 1989.

Lovejoy, Sharon. *Sunflower Houses.* Loveland, Colo.: Interweave Press, 1994.

———. *Hollyhock Days: Garden Adventures for the Young at Heart.* Colo.: Interweave Press, 1994.

Mallet, Robert. *Rebirth of a Park or Awakening Beauty.* Varengeville-sur-Mer, France: Centre d'Art Floral, 1996.

Margolin, Malcolm. *The Earth Manual: How to Work on Wildland without Taming It.* Berkeley, Calif.: Heyday Books, 1975.

Matthews, Caitlin. *Celtic Devotional: Daily Prayers and Blessings.* Hants, England: Godsfield Press, 1996.

May, Rollo. *The Courage to Create.* New York: W. W. Norton & Co., 1975.

Mellon, Nancy. *Storytelling and the Art of Imagination.* Rockport, Mass.: Element, 1992.

Morrison, Tony, ed. *Margaret Mee: In Search of Flowers in the Amazon Forests: Diaries of an English artist reveal the beauty of the vanishing rainforests.* Woodbridge, England: Nonesuch Expeditions Ltd., 1988.

Peterson, Bryan. *Learning to See Creatively.* New York: AMPHOTO, 1988.

Pipkin, James. *Places of Tranquility.* New York: Ballantine Books, 1990.

Pyle, Howard. *The Garden Behind the Moon.* New York: Parabola Books, 1988.

Royal Botanical Gardens, Kew. *A Vision of Eden: The Life and Work of Marianne North.* Devon, England: Webb & Bower, 1986.

Schinz, Marina. *Visions of Paradise: Themes and Variations on the Garden.* New York: Stewart, Tabori & Chang, 1979.

Solomon, Barbara Stauffacher. *Green Architecture and the Agrarian Garden.* New York: Rizzoli, 1988.

Stein, Sara. *Noah's Garden: Restoring the Ecology of Our Own Backyards.* Boston and New York: Houghton Mifflin Co., 1993.

———. *My Weeds: A Garden's Botany.* Boston and New York: Houghton Mifflin Co., 1988.

Stone, Curtis and Sharpe. *Every Part of This Earth is Sacred: Native American Voices in Praise of Nature.* San Francisco: Harper, 1993.

Thacker, Christopher. *The History of Gardens.* Berkeley, Calif.: UC Berkeley Press, 1979.

Thaxter, Celia. *An Island Garden.* New York: Houghton Mifflin, 1984.

Verey, Rosemary. *The Scented Garden: Choosing, growing and using the plants that bring fragrance to your life, home and table.* New York: Van Nostrand Reinhold, 1981.

Weeks, Sara T., and Bartlett Hayes Jr., eds. *Search for the Real and Other Essays by Hans Hofmann.* Cambridge, Mass.: MIT Press, 1986.

Wright, Machaelle Small. *Garden Workbook: A Complete Guide to Gardening with Nature Intelligences.* Warrenton, Va.: Perelandra, 1993.

Articles:

"Healing." *Parabola,* Vol. XVIII, no. 1, 1993

"Labyrinth." *Parabola,* Vol. XVII, no. 2, 1992.

"Sacred Space." *Parabola,* Vol. III, no. 1, 1978.

"The Soul." *Parabola,* Vol. XXI, no. 2, 1996.

Music:

Klein, Minra Devi. "Ragini—Fluted Voice of the Goddess" and "Ancient Future." Kentfield, Calif.: Bamboo Moon Musik.

Schroeder-Sheker, Terese. "Rosa Mystica" and "In Dulci Jubilo." Tucson, Ariz.: Celestial Harmonies, 1990, 1991.

Additional resources:

ARAS (Archive for Research in Archetypal Symbolism), 2040 Gough Street, San Francisco, Calif. 94109; telephone (415) 771-8055.

Breast Cancer Prayer Flag Tribute (a way to honor women who have faced breast cancer). 282 Second Street, Third Floor, San Francisco, Calif. 94105.

Perelandra, Ltd., Center for Nature Research, P.O. Box 3603, Warrenton, Va. 20188
Perelandra rose and garden essences can be ordered, as well as more books on working with the nature realm.

Mountain Gypsy Wildflowers Seminars, P.O. Box 503, Chicago Park, Calif. 95712. Enjoy wildflower hiking seminars with Julie Carville, author of *Lingering in Tahoe's Wild Gardens.*

Veriditas: The Greening Power of God, c/o Dr. Lauren Artress, Grace Cathedral, 1100 California Street, San Francisco, Calif. 94108.; telephone (415) 749-6356, FAX (415) 749-6357. This is a worldwide project to reintroduce the labyrinth as a spiritual tool and to help to create sacred communities around the globe. Write for their newsletter and information on pilgrimage walks, workshops, and seed kits.

Bibliography

Alexander, Christopher. *A Pattern Language.* Oxford: Oxford University Press, 1977.

———. *A Timeless Way of Building.* Oxford: Oxford University Press, 1979.

Andrews, Valerie. *A Passion for this Earth: Exploring a New Partnership of Man, Woman and Nature.* San Francisco: Harper, 1990.

Arrien, Angeles. *Signs of Life: The Five Universal Shapes and How to Use Them.* Sonoma, Calif.: Arcus Publishing, 1992.

Brown, Jane. Beatrix: *The Gardening Life of Beatrix Jones Farrand 1972–1959.* New York: Viking, 1995.

Campbell, Joseph. *The Power of Myth.* New York: Doubleday, 1988.

Coe, Ralph. *Sacred Circles: Two Thousand Years of North American Indian Art.* London: Arts Council of Great Britain, 1977.

Cook, Roger. *The Tree of Life: Image for the Cosmos.* New York: Avon Books, 1974.

Covarrubias, Miguel. *Island of Bali.* New York: Alfred Knopf, 1973.

Elseman, Fred B. Jr. *Bali Sekala & Niskala. Vols. I and II.* Bali: Fred B. Elseman Jr., 1990.

Francis, Mark, and Randolph T. Hester Jr., eds. *The Meaning of Gardens.* Cambridge, Mass.: MIT Press, 1990.

Ghyka, Matila. *The Geometry of Art and Life.* New York: Dover, 1977.

Gleick, James. *Chaos: Making a New Science.* New York: Penguin Books, 1987.

Grierson, Roderick, ed. *Gates of Mystery: The Art of Holy Russia.* Fort Worth, Tex.: Intercultura, n.d.

Grof, Stanislav and Christina. *Beyond Death: The Gates of Consciousness.* London: Thames & Hudson, 1980.

Hazelhurst, Hamilton F. *Gardens of Illusion: The Genius of André le Nostre.* Nashville, Tenn.: Vanderbilt University Press, 1980.

Henderson, Marjorie, and Elizabeth Wilkinson, eds. *Decorating Eden: A Comprehensive Sourcebook of Classic Garden Details.* San Francisco: Chronicle Books, 1992.

House, John. *Monet: Nature into Art.* New Haven: Yale University Press, 1986.

Huntley, H. E. *The Divine Proportion.* New York: Dover, 1970.

Itoh, Teiji. *Gardens of Japan.* Tokyo: Kodansha International, Ltd., 1984.

Jung, Carl. *Man and His Symbols.* New York: Doubleday, 1964.

Kandinsky, Wassily. *Concerning the Spiritual in Art.* New York: George Wittenborn, Inc., 1947.

Keswick, Maggie, Judy Oberlander, and Joe Wai. *In a Chinese Garden*. Vancouver, B.C.: Dr. Sun Yat-Sen Garden Society, 1990.

Koren, Leonard. *Wabi-Sabi for Artists, Designers, Poets and Philosophers*. Berkeley, Calif.: Stone Bridge Press, 1994.

Lacey, Stephen. *The Startling Jungle: Colour and Scent in the Romantic Garden*. New York: Viking Penguin, 1987.

Lawlor, Anthony, AIA. *The Temple in the House: Finding the Sacred in Everyday Architecture*. New York: G.P. Putnam's Sons, 1994.

Lawlor, Robert. *Sacred Geometry: Philosophy and Practice*. London: Thames & Hudson, 1982.

Lossky, Vladimir, and Leonid Ouspensky. *The Meaning of Icons*. Crestwood, N.Y.: St. Vladimir's Seminary Press, 1989.

Metropolitan Museum of Art. *A Chinese Garden Court*. New York: The Metropolitan Museum of Art, 1985.

Michell, John. *Earth Spirit: Its Ways, Shrines, and Mysteries*. New York: Avon Books, 1975.

Moore, Thomas. *Care of the Soul: A Guide for Cultivating Depth and Sacredness in Everyday Life*. New York: Harper Collins, 1992.

Mor, Barbara, and Monica Sjöö. *The Great Cosmic Mother: Rediscovering the Religion of the Earth*. San Francisco: Harper & Row, 1987.

Murray, Elizabeth. *Monet's Passion: Ideas, Inspiration and Insights from the Painter's Gardens*. San Francisco: Pomegranate Artbooks, 1989.

Nachmanovitch, Stephen. *Free Play: The Power of Improvisation in Life and the Arts*. Los Angeles: Jeremy P. Tarcher, Inc., 1990.

Osbon, Diane K., ed. *Reflections on the Art of Living; A Joseph Campbell Companion*. New York: Harper Perennial, 1991.

Osmen, Sarah Ann. *Sacred Places: A Journey into the Holiest Lands*. New York: St. Martins Press, 1990.

Palton, Bill. *Bali Handbook*. Chico, Calif.: Moon Publications, 1992.

Pereire, Anita, and Gabrielle Van Zuylen. *Gardens of France*. New York: Harmony, 1983.

Pepper, Elizabeth and John Wilcock. *A Guide to Magical & Mystical Sites: Europe and the British Isles*. San Francisco: Harper & Row, 1977.

Petrie, Flinders. *Decorative Patterns of the Ancient World*. New York: Crescent Books, 1990.

Purce, Jill. *The Mystic Spiral: Journey of the Soul*. New York: Avon Books, 1974.

Rossbach, Sarah. *Feng Shui: The Chinese Art of Placement*. New York: Viking Penguin, 1983.

————. *Interior Design with Feng Shui*. New York: Viking Penguin, 1987.

Sunset Books. *Western Garden Book*. Menlo Park, Calif.: Lane Publishing Co., 1988.

Valéry, Marie-Françoise. *Gardens in Normandy*. Paris and New York: Flammarion, 1995.

Welch, Stuart Cary. *Persian Painting: Five Royal*

Safavid Manuscripts of the Sixteenth Century. New York: George Braziller, 1976.

Weyl, Hermann. *Symmetry.* Princeton, N.J.: Princeton University Press, 1980.

Wright, Machaelle Small. *Flower Essences.* Jeffersonton, Va.: Perelandra, Ltd., 1988.

Yoshikawa, Isao, *Chine Gardens.* Tokyo: Graphic-sha Publishing Co., 1990.

Articles:

Anderson, William. "The Green Man." *Parabola: The Tree of Life.* Vol. XIV, no. 3., fall 1989.

Bruchac, Joseph. "Combing the Snakes from Atatarho's Hair." *Parabola: The Golden Mean.* Vol. XVI, no. 4, winter 1991.

Fitzgerald, Astrid. "Harmony by Design." *Parabola: The Golden Mean.* Vol. XVI, no. 4, winter 1991.

Hanh, Thich Nhat. "Peace Is Every Step." *Parabola: The Golden Mean.* Vol. XVI, no. 4, winter 1991.

Lawlor, Robert. "The Measure of Difference." *Parabola: The Golden Mean.* Vol. XVI, no. 4, winter 1991.

Luke, Helen. "Humility." *Parabola: The Golden Mean.* Vol. XVI, no. 4, winter 1991.

Travers, P. L. "The Celestial Root." *Parabola: The Tree of Life.* Vol. XIV, no. 3., fall 1989.

"Music's Discipline of the Means." *Parabola: The Golden Mean.* Vol. XVI, no. 4, winter 1991.

"The Golden Proportion." *Parabola: The Golden Mean.* Vol. XVI, no. 4, winter 1991.

Audiotapes:

O'Donohue, John. "Anam Cara: Wisdom from the Celtic World." Boulder, Colo.: Sounds True Audio.

Arrien, Angeles. "Gathering Medicine." Boulder, Colo.: Sounds True Audio.

Berry, Father Thomas. "Dawn over the Earth." Boulder, Colo.: Sounds True Audio.

Estes, Clarissa Pinkola. "The Faithful Gardener" Boulder, Colo.: Sounds True Audio.

————. "The Radiant Coat." Boulder, Colo.: Sounds True Audio.

————. "Women Who Run with the Wolves." Boulder, Colo.: Sounds True Audio.

Video:

Smithsonian Institution. "Dream Windows—A View to Japanese Gardens." Washington, D.C.: Smithsonian Institution.

Acknowledgments

I feel honored and happy to acknowledge all of my invaluable and supportive family, friends, guides, and teachers. Just as in Gerald's dream, where a pebble dropped into a pool of water creates radiating rings of energy and love, it is my wish that this book provides ripples of love and rewards for all who have contributed to its creation:

Ellie Rilla and Patrick Laherty, who have been with me through celebrations of life, death, and rebirth, always believing and always supporting; Sandy Rader, her architect husband, Terry Wilson—who drew our wedding garden for this book—and their children, Chloe and Michael—a family of love, color, creativity, celebration, fun, support, and play; Kathleen Burgy, the wisest and most wonderful youthful crone in the world;

Rebecca Murray, my beloved niece, teacher, and precious child; Dad, a loving supporter; my brothers—Thomas, who generously shares his archetypal knowledge; Jim, who has walked the spiritual path of Life-Death-Life with me; and Matt, who catches the Salmon of Wisdom and feeds it to all of us; my sisters, Cathrine and Mary, who pushed me to advocate and fight for Gerald's health; my darling nephew, Taylor Thomas, whose birth I witnessed; Uncle Fenton Kilkenny, who has told the stories of Bali since I was a child, and his wife, Leigh;

Kay Cline, a constant source of reflective listening and insights; Jeanne Cameron, who enriches my life with renewing retreats in Maine; Anna Rheim, photographer of precious moments who celebrates all depths of life;

Gerald's family: Morris, Kees, and Joor Bol, who offered love and support; and Josh, Jennifer, Chris, Sasha, Kaya, and Ashley, the new caretakers of Gerald's land—may you receive blessings from this sacred space;

Natalie and Rich Foster, who have always given me deep caring and wonderful food; Roelof, Virginia, Martha, and Jessica Wijbrandus, who have always kept faith, hope, and love; Marie Butcher, who helped me with my first manuscript, and her father, Rev. John Butcher, who married Gerald and me; artist Susan Dorf, who helped me paint my process; Elaine and Mark Schlegel, who have nurtured my inner and outer gardens with friendship and love; Yvonne Gorman, painter of the healing angel; Kay and Jill Smith, who brought back the beauty and light into my garden; Debra K. Davalos, a relentless source of enthusiastic cheer;

Pauline Kirby, my acupuncturist, friend, and

healer; Ed Jarvis, who aligns me toward my higher self; Anna Swartley, who always provides knowing counsel; Gerald's cancer support group and my hospice grief support group; Maria Lani, Hawaiian healer; Pam Austin, coach and cheerleader; Ellen Frelander, intuitive guide; Mara Freeman, who adds illumination;

Dennie, Alison and Mary, who shared Bali with me; Janet Ady, giver of love and empathy; Jesus Mora , who helped Gerald and me make our garden; John Dotson, who has always recognized the sacred in gardens; Ray Davi, who lit a candle at every mission in California while Gerald was ill; Joe Long, always cheering; Emery Jones, who emanates deep knowing and acceptance; Elsa and Sam Knoll, shining elder examples; Thomas Gröner and Ziglinda, who wove their love and beauty into magical flower bouquets for our wedding; Lyn Sweeney, who uses the power of photography for healing and remembrance; Toolie and Snow White, who make me laugh, walk, and heal;

All the garden makers in this book: the monks at Kokedera Temple; the people of Bali; the Rockefeller family; Claude Monet and the keepers of his gardens, from Mr. Vahi and the garden team to director Mme. Lindsey and the curators, M. and Mme. Vanderkemp; the creators and keepers of Esalen; Mark Brown; Mary Holmes; Hank Helbush and Rebecca Dye; Betty and Willis Peck and their daughter, Annie, and granddaughters Sara and Marinia; Gerald Bol; and Lily Yeh;

Robin Goodfellow, who with her skillful hand and tiny scissors created the delightful apple tree silhouettes; Nan Perrott, who with saintly patience typed my handwritten, held-together-with-tape manuscript into a whole; and Katie and Tom Burke, who always believed and waited with love through the dormant time until fruition.